1993

Student Publications

Legalities, Governance, and Operation

Student

 IOWA STATE UNIVERSITY PRESS / AMES

Publications

Legalities, Governance, and Operation

LOUIS EDWARD INGELHART

Louis E. Ingelhart is Professor Emeritus of Journalism and Director Emeritus of Student Publications at Ball State University, Muncie, Indiana.

© 1993 Iowa State University Press, Ames, Iowa 50010. All rights reserved

Manufactured in the United States of America
⊗ This book is printed on acid-free paper.

First edition, 1993

Library of Congress Cataloging-in-Publication Data

Ingelhart, Louis E. (Louis Edward)
    Student publications : legalities, governance, and operation / Louis Edward Ingelhart. — 1st ed.
        p.   cm.
    Includes bibliographical references and index.
    ISBN 0-8138-1478-2 (alk. paper)
    1. College student newspapers — United States. 2. College student newspapers — Law and legislation — United States. I. Title.
LB3621.65.I54   1993
378.1′9897 — dc20   90-27874

TO A. M. "Sandy" Sanderson and John A. Boyd,
the first executive secretaries who served the
National Council of College Publications Advisers
for many years before that pioneer organization
became College Media Advisers, Inc.

CONTENTS

PREFACE

This book about college student publications has been prepared and issued under the auspices of the Press Law Committee of College Media Advisers (CMA), Inc. It began in 1971 when a CMA research committee undertook a legal study of who could be considered as publishers of student publications in public colleges and universities.

In the midst of this study, a series of articles in newspapers and magazines appeared extolling the virtues of incorporating student publications, cutting off college funds, and moving the publications off campus so they could be independent of host colleges and thus exercise unrestrained press freedom.

College Media Advisers was appalled by these articles because a serious application of their recommendations would bankrupt and destroy 90 percent of the college student publications. CMA had been monitoring court decisions that established quite firmly that the First Amendment guarantee of press freedom protected the free expression of student journalists under the leadership of the student editor, narrowed the traditional publisher role for university officials under provisions of the Fourteenth Amendment, and indicated that funding by the colleges could not be the basis for content controls.

College Media Advisers issued a position paper in the form of a 20-page tabloid to refute the articles. Each year a few additional student publications do become incorporated, but more than 95 percent have retained their organizational structure within the college and with college funding.

Since the tabloid's issuance, student publications in some public and private colleges have had difficulties in financing and funding, and have faced efforts at censorship by repressive officials or student governments. Fortunately, however, most colleges endorse the operation of a free student press.

By 1980 all of the copies of the tabloid had been sold or distributed. Harassment and pressures on several college student publications beginning in the 1980s alerted several advisers and student staff members to ask for materials to restock their protective arsenals.

They did have available to them a series of College Media Publications materials, books on student press law, the helpful services of a

Student Press Law Center, a revitalized Associated Collegiate Press, and the Collegiate Division of the Columbia Scholastic Press Association. But the student publications wanted and needed more.

While serving as chairman of the journalism department at Eastern Illinois University, I became chairman of the Press Law Committee of College Media Advisers and found awaiting requests for a reissue of the tabloid. The press law committee decided instead that that material was due for considerable updating to reflect decisions in hundreds of law cases and developments in technology and higher education.

I enlisted Louis E. Ingelhart, who was the principal author of the original tabloid, to launch an updating. This book is the product of a collaborative discussion among the committee, additional publications advisers, and attorneys—as well as research and writing efforts of Dr. Ingelhart and editing contributions from me and James Tidwell, an attorney and a professor of journalism law at Eastern Illinois University.

It is presented by College Media Advisers and its Press Law Committee for use by student publications persons, educational administrators, and others. It contains a thorough description of the nature and function of student publications in both public and private colleges. We hope it will be used to promote or develop environments for free and vigorous student publications on those campuses.

John David Reed
Press Law Committee of College Media Advisers, Inc.

INTRODUCTION

College Media Advisers, Inc., is a national organization of professionals dedicated to the improvement of the quality of student publications in American colleges through skillful advising and teaching. This purpose can be achieved if colleges and universities—private and public alike—maintain an atmosphere of freedom for the campus student press. Arrangements for an adequate and stable financial base for their operation and provision for adequate space and technology would also be helpful.

The adviser's role is to provide continuity for each student publication, including the maintenance of an accurate and complete financial records system. Many advisers have succeeded admirably in this role.

There are handicaps and problems, however. University administrative officials frequently become frightened or dismayed by the content of student publications and can easily decide to restrain or control that content. Financing student publications is an endless task. Recruiting and training competent student staff members can be frustrating. In the midst of all this hard work and sensitive people, every few years detractors—on or off campus—launch an anti–student publications offensive. College Media Advisers attempts to meet those challenges whenever possible with explanatory publications and activities to set the record straight. This book is one such effort under the auspices of the Student Press Law Committee of College Media Advisers.

The 1960s were the dark ages of American campus journalism, just as the early 1800s were the dark ages of American journalism. Newspapers of that era were captives of the political wars of that age; their record of bias and political chicanery made them unreliable as communications media. The 1960s were the days of the campus underground press. Journalism educators scurried away from the obscene, strident, foul, biased, and nasty publications that created a stench on campuses everywhere. Newspapers, magazines, and even yearbooks were caught up in this tumultuous time. College administrators and board members were aghast and frightened by it.

So they ran too. They tried discipline. They tried cutting off funds. They tried everything they could think of to escape the effects of that press and any involvement in it. Nothing worked. Litigation marched through courts of the land and proclaimed over and over again that the First Amendment applied to all, even foul-typewritered campus journalists.

College administrators faced another problem. Money began to run out. Inflation began having an effect, and stinginess of state legislatures caused misery everywhere. Dismay and poverty motivated administrators to try to do something.

They realized that administrators, teachers, and advisers in public institutions could not control the content of the student press. No such individual could serve as publisher of the campus student press. Nor could the university reduce or abolish funding because of dissatisfaction with the content of the campus press. Court decisions reiterated this time after time.

During the 1980s, the United States contained approximately 3,600 college campuses. On these campuses there were more than 3,000 student newspapers, nearly 2,000 yearbooks, and at least 1,800 magazines or other student publications. Circulations of these student publications approached 25 million copies annually, and expenditures approached $150 million as the decade ended. There were hundreds of other types of publications produced by student staff and hundreds of student-operated radio stations on the air. There were even student television stations. That's big business and big journalism.

More than 90 percent of the colleges had student newspapers, more than one-half had student yearbooks, and nearly half had magazines or other publications. More than 90 percent of the newspapers and magazines, and nearly 80 percent of the yearbooks, were financed entirely, primarily, or partially by allocations from college general funds or from mandatory student fees. Thus, only a minority were financed entirely outside college funding.

In the United States, higher education is part of the philosophical system outlined in the Constitution of the nation. The human freedoms and rights grandly enumerated in that document parallel the purposes and goals of education. College administrators, teachers, and board members are realizing that espousal of a free press, with its imperfections, hoopla, and stridency, provides great learning for the practical journalist and the campus reader alike. It is the best practical example and exercise of what the tussle of thinking and learning is all about. It is almost impossible to teach thinking, learning, testing, experimenting, mistaking, achieving, creating, and knowing in the sequester called a classroom and then deny any public evidence that such things might be occurring on the campus among the students. The campus press is a clarion demonstration of the university's being a university doing the work of a university. As such it belongs on the campus, in the catalog, and in the budget.

The campus press has had a turbulent history following World War II. In the late 1940s and early 1950s came a period of getting started again, aided by the formation of College Media Advisers and the positive contributions of students on the GI bill.

The 1950s, with huge enrollment growth, pushed campus journalism forward faster than it was prepared to develop. Many student editors and advisers found out what hard work and long hours really were.

The 1960s became a time of national disillusionment that certainly embroiled the campus press, which deteriorated into something incorrectly labeled the underground press.

The 1970s saw great growth in journalism education enrollments and the arrival of offset, phototype, and computer production, budget constraints, and inflation.

By the 1980s, much of the philosophical dislocation of the 1960s and 1970s had been overcome, but the problems of inflation were becoming more difficult to handle. If that inflation can be managed, the 1990s can become a golden age for the campus press with the utilization of the newer technology and the greater skills and dedication of campus journalists.

This book appears at this time partly in response to a recent publication titled *Enhancing Relationships with the Student Press*[1] which unfortunately contributes to the confusion undermining college student publications. The booklet, edited by John H. Schuh, is part of a series for student services published by Jossey-Bass, Inc., for the use of student personnel or affairs officers. Editor Schuh presents materials prepared by several writers in an effort to make relationships better. Unfortunately, this effort fails.

C. Peter Magrath, president of the University of Missouri, outlines a presidential perspective of student publications. It is not clear whether he wrote his comments before or after he led the University of Minnesota as its president into a $183,000 loss in the Eighth Circuit Court of Appeals when the *Minnesota Daily* successfully won reinstatement of its full student fees arrangements and thus overcame an episode of restraint for content punishment. The court said the motivation of the university was unconstitutional no matter how eloquent its defense might be.

By far the least acceptable chapter in the Schuh book is one written by Jon C. Dalton in which he postulates the necessity of student affairs officers developing the moral and ethical personalities of student publications staff members. Any student affairs person who would attempt to impose the specific actions proposed by Dalton would be laughed from the room by every student journalist. His proposals would not stand constitutional scrutiny in the courts.

Stuart F. Hayes attempts an annotated bibliography, which demonstrates why some student affairs officers have difficulty understanding a field many of them have administrative responsibilities for. Hayes does not cite a number of articles that have appeared in *College Media Review* when it was still called *College Press Review.*[2] He includes the Duscha and Fischer book on *The Campus Press,*[3] which is considered a weak, and perhaps dangerous, volume by most college student publications advisers. He mentions the old Ingelhart study for College Media Advisers on *The College and University Student Press,*[4] which is woefully out-of-date. Even more out-of-date is the Stevens and Webster *Law and the Student Press.*[5]

Discussions of the college student press should include as a basic source *Law of the Student Press,*[6] produced by the Student Press Law Center in 1985 and revised in 1988, or the Ingelhart book on *Freedom for the College Student Press,*[7] also published in 1985.

A reading of the Schuh book will find at least 137 directives mandating student publication staff members to do or not to do something. Since these pertain to content, the courts would rule against student personnel officers of public colleges who would seriously attempt to impose or administer the directives. The tone of the book is generally conciliatory and reflects an eagerness to help the student journalist, but on terms advantageous to the student affairs officer and the college.

The book is too much oriented to the sophisticated student programs found in large universities. The Duscha and Fischer book made the same mistake by looking at student newspapers in 10 universities, none of which was typical of America's 3,600 colleges and universities. The Duscha portion of the book aroused College Media Advisers to issue a 20-page refutation that was angry, shrill, and unkind. Julius Duscha is actually one of the kindest and most supportive persons a student journalist could ever know, but College Media Advisers flailed away vigorously at his book regarding topics that appear subsequently in this book.

Indeed, this report is primarily an updating of the 1973 College Media Advisers tabloid. This updated version is partly inspired by the Jossey-Bass booklet of 1986 and by a recognition that an overall look at college student publications might be helpful even though doctrinaire or controversial. Not all college student publications advisers agree with what follows. I hope the material will be of use, maybe merely as a catalyst to dig deeper and think more wisely about college student publications.

Louis E. Ingelhart

Student Publications
Legalities, Governance, and Operation

CHAPTER 1

Mythmaking

Mythmaking has surrounded the campus student press throughout past decades. The mythmakers are mostly educators or professional journalists who happen by the campus press world, take a quick look, and then write an article or book. Occasionally, they are joined by student journalists or even a few college advisers who parade "independence." Initial reports in the 1970s were largely small items tucked into such publications as *Editor and Publisher* reporting that some campus newspapers had incorporated to become independent of their host universities.

Publications advisers with considerable knowledge of these campuses chuckled at the misinformation briefly and ignored the little reports. But a plethora of myths and mythmakers changed all of that.

In 1971 College Media Advisers appointed an ad hoc research committee to evaluate the legal status of the campus student press. Much of the data this committee collected refuted many of the myths; a look at some of the myths and their perpetrators outlined the dimensions of a possible dilemma in which university officials can be trapped. In 1966 College Media Advisers authorized Dr. Dario Politella, its president, to conduct a two-year study of the status of college student publications in America. Politella assembled a commission on the Freedoms and Responsibilities of the College Student Press in America to perform this study. The study used the 15–member commission, a survey of 72 colleges, and correspondence, conversations, and visits to campuses by Politella.[1]

He produced a set of guidelines that became the basis of a report published by *Seminar* quarterly as a full-length supplement in December 1969. His guidelines:

1. A student press that is relevant to its campus makes service its ideal purpose.

2. A self-regulated student press is a free student press.

3. A responsible student press should reasonably be expected to maintain a level of professional performance and ethics pertinent to its purpose and restricted by its resources.

4. Financial independence is a cornerstone of true freedom and responsibility of the student press.

5. The role of the student press adviser is to help students to transfer their theories to practice.

6. The free student press is free to all who have something worth saying.

In these guidelines, Politella did not recommend that activity money be cut from student publications but that such allocations be considered legitimate circulation income.

Politella's guidelines were not adopted by College Media Advisers; unfortunately, some of the mythmakers used distortions of Politella's report as a basis for attacks on the campus press.

Typical of mythmakers were paragraphs tucked in at the end of an *Editor and Publisher* article published March 3, 1973. The article reported that the *Stanford Daily* had become independent from its private university and that its editor was no longer afraid of censorship or fee cutoffs by the student government. Then *Editor and Publisher* enlarged the myth by reporting:

> Student newspapers that have reorganized on an independent basis in recent years include the *Daily Californian* at Berkeley, the University of Kentucky *Kernel,* the University of Oregon *Daily Emerald,* and the Florida State *Flambeau.*
>
> Campuses where independence was under study included the University of Florida and the University of Arkansas.
>
> College newspapers with a long history of editorial and financial independence included the Cornell *Daily Sun,* the *Daily Dartmouth,* the *Harvard Crimson,* and the *University of Michigan Daily,* and the *Yale Daily News.*[2]

Actually, only 2 of the 12 college newspapers mentioned in the article could claim independence.

Six months earlier Fred M. Hechinger was mythmaking in the *New York Times.* He reported that the *Stanford Daily* was becoming independent rather than remain a part of the university structure. It thus joined independently operated student papers such as the *Harvard Crimson,* the Cornell *Daily Sun,* the *Yale Daily News,* the *Daily*

Californian at Berkeley, and several others that were immune from administrative or faculty supervision.

Although Hechinger cautioned bankruptcy for independent publications, he listed these advantages for supposed independence:

1. The independent paper must earn the confidence and support of its readers and is therefore under constraint to be more professional in its approach.

2. Independence makes efficient operations essential to survival and also makes student journalism a better training ground for news media careers.

3. Without the university as a protecting shield, student editors are more aware of the danger of libel.

4. The independent student paper tends to enjoy greater credibility among students who do not suspect it of being a public relations tool of the administration.[3]

Hechinger cited no evidence to support these statements.

At a point further back in time, Noel Greenwood, a *Los Angeles Times* reporter, and the headline writer for *Quill* magazine built a myth when reporting the independence of the *Daily Californian* at Berkeley.[4] Greenwood played the illusion of independence, while the headline writer suggested others would follow the lead of that perennial trendsetter, California. The myth flew on the wings of the LA Times–Washington Post News Service to its newspaper subscribers.

Perry Sorenson reported to the *National Observer* that a roomful of mythmakers met in Washington to talk independence for the campus press. He suggested that college presidents can escape embarrassment by merely kicking student newspapers into an "independence" limbo.

The trend toward independence, including the best ways to go about it, was one of the main discussion topics for officials of large state schools at an annual meeting of the National Association of State Universities and Land Grant Colleges. Independence, most agreed, results in more subdued publications. The stories, pictures, and ads that cause administrators so many headaches usually disappear.

"It doesn't take long for the student to learn what every country editor knows," said Glenwood L. Creech, then vice president of the University of Kentucky. "You can't kick the owner of the five-and-dime store in the pants every week and expect him to advertise in your paper."

Creech directed the one-year transition of the University of Kentucky *Kernel* from a paper partly supported by student funds to one with financial independence.

"When they were getting the student money, the *Kernel* staff would sell just enough ads to get through the year," says Creech. "Then they'd do as they damn well pleased the rest of the time.

"There are some who think the paper was more exciting in those days," says Creech, "but my life has been a hell of a lot more pleasant since we made the change. I knew it was a thorn, but I didn't know how big a thorn it was until they pulled it out."[5]

Student staff members believed the move to what they called independence was done for positive reasons, not as an administrative cop-out. Creech maintained an interesting track record with the campus press. *Editor and Publisher* reported in its October 13, 1973, issue that Florida Atlantic University at Boca Raton had a tussle between Creech and the *Atlantic Sun*. Here's what happened.

In their first issue of the semester the editors charged that the new president, Dr. Glenwood Creech, who came from the University of Kentucky, was stopping dissemination of sex education materials. The article was illustrated with a rear picture of two nudes that appeared on the cover of an abortion brochure.

Dr. Creech denied the accuracy of the story and criticized the editors' judgment in printing the picture of nudes. He offered the *New York Times* and the *Miami Herald* as examples of better journalism, suggesting the students might emulate them.

In their next issue the students retorted by printing a *New York Times* photograph of naked youths at the Woodstock Rock Festival in 1971. "President Creech is wrong," said the *Sun* editorial. "Today's *Times* carries a photograph which certainly showed more flesh than the *Sun* picture. So you do find nude pictures in 'more responsible' publications."

In his *National Observer* article, Sorenson listed other "independent" papers as the *Flambeau* of Florida State, the *Alligator* of the University of Florida, the *Daily Emerald* of the University of Oregon, the *Daily* at Stanford, the *Traveler* of the University of Arkansas, the *Spectator* of Columbia University, the *Crimson* of Harvard University, and the *Daily* of the University of Michigan. Sorenson almost escaped the mythmaker label by raising several questions and cautions about the advantages of independence. Actually only one of his nine papers had a strong claim to real independence.

The *Kentucky Kernel* issue of December 13 carried a full-page "house ad" to recruit staff members that proclaimed, "We are proud of our independence." The ad boasted: "A year ago today, the last University-subsidized issue of the *Kentucky Kernel* rolled off the presses of the UK Division of Printing. And a year after that, we remain the only totally independent university-sanctioned newspaper at a state university in the country."[6]

The *Florida Independent Alligator* was declared independent under peculiar circumstances that caused students to march on the home of the university president. The march was led by the student senate, which opposed the new arrangement.[7]

The *Chronicle of Higher Education* managed to turn a well-conceived article by Teresa L. Ebert into a myth by headlining it "More Papers Cutting Ties with Colleges — but with Some Misgivings."[8] Ebert mentioned eight college newspapers; clearly, she indicated that four were not independent, and only four might be. None really is. An editor placed a sidebar story with the Ebert article. It was based on a survey of the contents of 200 newspapers conducted by Herman Estrin, then an adviser to the New Jersey Collegiate Press Association. The Estrin survey clearly established that college newspapers published articles that covered almost every subject. No content restraints could have been in operation for these newspapers. But the *Chronicle* decided that Estrin's article should be interpreted with this headline: "Study Finds Many Officials Growing Weary of Problems Student Newspapers Generate."

These examples of mythmaking constitute an indicative sample of articles that have been, are, and probably will be published about the campus press. Articles in the 1980s, however, were more accurate and clear.

Perhaps the most curious analysis of the campus press was a report[9] by Julius Duscha, director of the Washington Journalism Center,[10] and by Thomas Fischer, a former assistant dean of the Georgetown University Law Center. The report was funded through a grant from The John and Mary R. Markle Foundation to the American Association of State Colleges and Universities (AASCU).

A national advisory committee on the student press, chaired by Thomas McGrath, president of California State College at Sonoma, worked with Duscha and Fischer on the project. Other members of the committee were Kathy Fraze, editor of the Bowling Green (Ohio) University *BG News;* Hillier Krieghbaum, professor emeritus of journalism at New York University and a past president of the Association for Education in Journalism; Richard J. Nelson, president of Northern Illinois University; Guy Ryan, assistant managing editor of the *San Diego Evening Tribune* and a past president of the Society of Professional Journalists; James Bond, president of California State University at Sacramento; and Owen R. Houghton, consultant for special projects for AASCU. The report was issued as a book titled *The Campus Press: Freedom and Responsibility.*

Duscha's principal conclusion was that "an independent student newspaper is obviously the best answer to the problems of the student press." Fischer attempted to be a courteous coauthor, but he had difficulties in supporting the thesis. Indeed, the legal review and cases he presented in the second half of the book contradicted it. Fischer took a retrospective look at its contents and prepared the following statement for the 1973 national convention of College Media Advisers:

> With regard to the legal status of the campus press as presented in my half of the recent AASCU publication, *The Campus Press: Freedom and Responsibility,* I want to make a few points absolutely clear. First, I do not advocate any particular form of student press, "independent" or otherwise. Realistically, not every college would want, or could afford, to separate its student press from institutional support and functions. I have attempted to indicate the form and legal status of several types of student publications without "advocating" any of them.
>
> I do advocate, however, that institutions do, and continue to, support and sponsor student publications. This is due to my feeling that these forms of activity—curricularly and extra-curricularly—constitute a valuable experience for the student and provide a generally useful forum for the college. Secondly, I strongly advocate that *whatever* publication structure is decided upon by an institution and its students—that decision being strictly local option—that the decision be *clearly spelled out* and not later ignored, twisted or arrogated by either party. Thirdly, I believe that *legally* that restraint of student publications is difficult to meet. The easiest to meet, of course, is obscenity. But the recent University of Missouri case indicates that even these standards are nearly impossible to meet under normal publishing grounds. Lastly, I would like to suggest that the most successful approach to campus press problems—one at least as viable as "independence"—is fair and mature dealing. Because college journals and journalists have been treated as miniatures of the real thing, they have behaved that way. If the matter was approached in a more mature and professional manner by the institution, I believe college journalists would respond in kind.

Anyone discussing the college student press should mention these and other agencies:

1. The National Council of College Publications Advisers, now called College Media Advisers, which is the only national faculty or-

ganization serving the field of student publications.

2. The Student Press Law Center.

3. The Associated Collegiate Press, a service organization contracted by College Media Advisers to provide rating and critique services, a magazine, a national convention, and other services to college newspapers, yearbooks, and magazines.

4. The Columbia Scholastic Press Association, another service organization also contracted by College Media Advisers to maintain a College Division and provide rating and critique services and a national convention.

John Behrens at Utica College maintains extensive archives of the student press for College Media Advisers.

It may be true that the earliest campus publications depended entirely upon advertising and subscriptions. Some were produced outside the purview of the university; others were not. Colleges and universities found that economical and stable financing of a host of activities could be accomplished with a low, universal student activity fee. If such a fee were not used, many colleges simply could not have publications. About 75 percent of the nation's colleges, big or small, public or private, found this system of financing student publications most practical. So the usual method of financing student publications is partially through a student activity fee or through an allocation of college funds.

Studies conducted by College Media Advisers and the Associated Collegiate Press over many years indicate that most college publications rely on several sources of income. Advertising produces considerable revenue for most college newspapers. Actually, allocations from student activity fees, which are the equivalent of the commercial newspaper's subscriptions, constitute only a part of most campus newspaper income. Many campus newspapers have considerable income from job printing, as do commercial newspapers.

Thomas Fischer utilized the second half of the book to review laws touching on aspects of the campus press. His work could be helpful since he had accumulated a handy listing of some of the early legal cases involving student publications. By law, every advantage and right proposed for an "independent" press now belong to each and every campus student publication currently being published in the United States in public colleges. If the First Amendment doesn't make this clear, the Fourteenth does.

Here are a series of statements made by Fischer, with the pages of *The Campus Press: Freedom and Responsibility* indicated:

A public institution will not be protected in the censorship of its student publications, although it insists that they are house organs or teaching vehicles, if the evidence reveals that these publications have not been restricted to these functions or managed according to the models discussed (pp. 61–62).

It is fairly well established that a college or university is not *legally* the "publisher" of the student publications which it sponsors, and may not censor or unduly influence the contents of those publications, directly or indirectly (p. 63).

It is clear, however, that the university administration is not legally the "publisher" of the campus newspaper (p. 64).

The Internal Revenue Service stated that "[the] expression of editorial opinion on political and legislative matters would appear to be an accepted feature of legitimate student newspapers." Thus, student newspapers would not jeopardize their tax exempt status by endorsing political candidates (p. 65).

It might be noted here that censorship in any form is equally reprehensible to the courts (p. 68).

The type of support and supervision supplied by the university is unimportant, so long as it is not applied in a discriminatory fashion or used as a censorship device (pp. 70–71).

As to the case law concerning a *university's* liability for defamation contained in a student article—as distinguished from the *student's* liability there-for—it is sparse indeed. No cases had been found by the 1970s (p. 79). [Subsequent cases have excused universities or colleges from such liability.]

Melvin Mencher, a Columbia University professor of journalism, said in an article in the *College Media Review:*[11]

> The courts over the past half-dozen years have consistently ruled in favor of student freedom. Today, it is clear that: The university is not legally the publisher of the campus newspaper, the newspaper cannot be censored, student editors cannot be summarily dismissed for their writings and the courts' ruling of libel and obscenity for the general, commercial press apply to the college press also.
>
> In short, a college professor or regent has no more power over the college newspaper published on a state-supported campus than President Nixon has over the *Washington Post.*

Since the university seemingly must be host to an organism it cannot control, the reasonable expectation would be for a search to seek a new relationship that would be mutually enriching while still recognizing the essential adversary relationship between press and power.

Instead, some universities are reacting to the new freedom by seeking a divorce. They want to divest themselves of their campus newspapers.

The device they have discovered is financial independence. Under this arrangement, the newspaper is no longer financed through subsidy or student activity fee. Newspaper offices are off-campus. When they are on-campus, the newspaper pays for everything: rent, utilities, maintenance.

A handful of newspapers have operated under financial independence, most of them in the Ivy League and in large campuses. Several have been financially independent for many years, and a few have taken this step within the past few years, usually after friction with campus administrations.

The Press Law Committee of College Media Advisers selected 12 court decisions that have had great impact in establishing a free press for student publications in public colleges. Following are summaries of the 12 cases.

Dickey v. *Alabama State Board of Education,* 273 F. Supp. 613 (M.D. Ala. 1967), was the first instance of a court's recognizing the First Amendment rights of college journalists. Gary Dickey, the editor of the student newspaper at Troy State University, printed the word "censored" in place of an editorial he was ordered not to run by his adviser and the school president.

The editorial he wanted to run was critical of the governor and the state legislature. However, the university had a rule prohibiting criticism of state officials.

When Dickey ran the word "censored" instead of a suggested substitute story about "Raising Dogs in North Carolina," the president suspended Dickey from the university for "insubordination."

A U.S. district court in Alabama ordered Dickey reinstated as a student, ruling that the college could not punish him for exercising his constitutional rights of free expression. The court said the rule against criticism of state officials was "unreasonable" and was not relevant to the "maintenance of order and discipline" on campus.

In *Antonelli* v. *Hammond,* 308 F. Supp. 1329 (D. Mass. 1970), the editor of the student newspaper at Fitchburg (Mass.) State College sued the college president for violating his First and Fourteenth Amendment rights. He claimed the president was censoring the material for publication by subjecting it to the prior approval of a faculty advisory committee and by refusing to release the money to pay for a particular issue because he disagreed with its content.

The court ruled in favor of the student. It said administrators cannot require prior submission to an advisory board and that college officials cannot censor expression they dislike.

Trujillo v. *Love,* 322 F. Supp. 1266 (D. Colo. 1971), was a case in which the managing editor of the student newspaper at Southern Colorado State University had been suspended from her position after censorship disagreements with the paper's faculty adviser. She brought suit claiming her First Amendment rights were violated.

The court ruled in the student's favor and ordered her reinstated as managing editor. It found the student newspaper was a public forum for student expression, and even though the university paid for the publication, officials could not place limitations upon the use of that forum where those limitations interfered with protected speech and were not justified by an overriding state interest. "The state is not necessarily the unfettered master of all it creates," the court said.

The decision in *Bazaar* v. *Fortune,* 476 F.2d 570, 489 F.2d 225 (5th Cir. 1973), cert. denied 414 U.S. 1135 (1973), enunciated early judicial doctrines that are now well established in college press case law. The court found (1) that the fact that the University of Mississippi, a state school, provided funding, faculty or departmental advice, or campus facilities did not authorize university officials to censor the content of a student publication (in this case a literary magazine); (2) that individual four-letter words were insufficient reasons to censor; (3) that the university could not be considered the same as a private publisher with absolute arbitrary powers to decide what could be printed; (4) that the university, as an arm of the state, could not make private publisher decisions about content and had infringed upon the free press rights of the students when it denied distribution rights to an issue of the magazine that contained articles about interracial love and Black pride; and (5) that the university could not be held liable for the content of student publications.

In *Joyner* v. *Whiting,* 447 F.2d 456 (4th Cir. 1973), a federal appellate court ruled that a state university cannot withdraw funding from a campus newspaper even when the newspaper editorializes in favor of racial segregation contrary to the Fourteenth Amendment and the 1964 Civil Rights Act. The president of North Carolina Central University had withdrawn funding from the paper and thus violated the First Amendment free press guarantees of students in a predominately black college who editorialized against integrating white students into the university. The court found that the proper remedy against censorship is restraint of the censor, not suppression of the press. It ruled that a state college could not impose censorship by asserting any form of censorial oversight, including attempts to exercise financial controls over a student publication because of the editorial stance.

Papish v. *Board of Curators of the University of Missouri,* 410 U.S. 667 (1973), involved a graduate student (Barbara Papish) at the University of Missouri who distributed on campus an "underground" newspaper that included a reprint of a political cartoon depicting policemen raping the Statue of Liberty and the Goddess of Justice. The newspaper also contained several four-letter words. Papish was expelled from the university for distributing a newspaper "containing forms of indecent speech."

The U.S. Supreme Court reversed and ordered her reinstatement because the university's action was not justified as a nondiscriminatory application of reasonable rules governing conduct. "The mere dissemination of ideas—no matter now offensive to good taste—on a state university campus may not be shut off in the name alone of 'conventions of decency,'" the Court said. It noted that the material in the newspaper was not constitutionally obscene or otherwise unprotected.

In *Schiff* v. *Williams,* 519 F.2d 257 (5th Cir. 1975), three editors of the student newspaper at Florida Atlantic University had been removed from their positions by the university president because of his perception of the quality of the paper, including poor grammar and spelling, "vilification and rumor mongering," and editorials that were "immature and unsophisticated diatribes." The editors filed a lawsuit against the president, and the court ordered the reinstatement of the editors. The court noted that none of the complaints raised by the president overcame the First Amendment rights of the student editors to make their own content decisions without school interference.

Mississippi Gay Alliance v. *Goudelock,* 536 F.2d 1073 (5th Cir. 1976), cert. denied 430 U.S. 982 (1977), resulted after the student editor of the Mississippi State University newspaper refused to run an advertisement from a campus gay organization. The organization sued, asking that the newspaper be forced to run its ad.

The Fifth Circuit Court of Appeals upheld the right of the student editor to make an editorial judgment on the choice of materials to go into the newspaper. It said the editor's refusal to run the advertisement was not government action, and therefore the First Amendment prohibited judicial interference with the decision of an editor.

Kania v. *Fordham,* 702 F.2d 475 (4th Cir. 1983), was a suit brought by several students at the University of North Carolina. They claimed that mandatory student fees that went to support the campus newspaper violated their First and Fourteenth Amendment rights. Through the fees, the students said, the state was forcing them to subsidize a publication even though they disagreed with many of its editorial positions.

The court ruled against the students, saying their constitutional rights were only minimally and indirectly restricted by the funding scheme and that the newspaper increased the overall exchange of information, ideas, and opinions on campus. The court also said the university could not compel the student newspaper to provide equal access to those disagreeing with its editorial positions without running afoul of the Constitution.

In *Milliner* v. *Turner,* 436 So. 2d 1300 (La. App. 1983), two faculty members of Southern University of New Orleans sued three editors of the school's newspaper for libel when they were described as a "proven fool" and "racist" in editorials. The students asked that the university be joined as a party to the suit. A trial court found both the student editors and the school responsible for libel.

The school appealed, claiming it could not be held responsible for the actions of its students. The state appellate court agreed. "[T]he choice of the content of material to go into the paper is an exercise of editorial control and judgment, and regulation of this crucial process [by school officials] would be inconsistent with the First Amendment guarantees of a free press," the court said. The First Amendment barred the school from anything other than advisory control over the student newspaper, so the school was exempt from any liability for the newspaper's libels.

The *Stanley* v. *Magrath,* 719 F.2d 279 (8th Cir. 1983), decision developed a legal doctrine authorizing analysis of the motivation of university administrators who had moved to restrict university funding of a student newspaper. Previously, it had been relatively easy for administrators to contend fund reductions were not made to control or punish editorial content, an argument difficult to refute until courts began to allow as evidence attacks made by administrators and trustees on publication content. After just such attacks on the University of Minnesota's student daily over a spoof issue, the federal court ruled that an ensuing change in the paper's student fee support structure, which was authorized by university trustees and which threatened to reduce the paper's financial support, was an unconstitutional attempt to punish the newspaper.

Sinn v. *The Daily Nebraskan,* 829 F.2d 662 (8th Cir. 1987), aff'g

638 F. Supp. 143 (D. Neb. 1986), involved two individuals in the University of Nebraska community who had sought to place in the school's newspaper advertisements seeking roommates and noting their sexual orientation. The editor rejected the ads, saying they suggested an intent to discriminate against individuals who were not gay or lesbian. The potential advertisers sued the student newspaper, the University of Nebraska, and other school officials, claiming that the rejection of their ads by the state-funded student newspaper was an infringement of their First Amendment rights. Two federal courts disagreed, holding that the First Amendment protects only against actions of state actors, those acting under the authority of the government. Because the student editor made the decision to reject the ads in question without any force from school officials or the school's publications board and because his decision was protected by the First Amendment, the court said, the advertisers' First Amendment rights were not infringed.

There are many additional court cases that have been decided in favor of student free press in public colleges. Very little litigation has occurred involving student publications in private colleges. From the first significant case in 1967 until the late 1980s, there has been a parade of pro–free press decisions. Persons writing in the early 1970s did not have this legal record to assist them, and colleges have had to retreat from press restraints during the last 15 years.

As a result very few myths or mythmakers were in evidence in the latter part of the 1970s or in the early 1980s, but as the 1980s rushed toward the 1990s, there did appear newcomers who repeated some of the lightweight views. Some advocated strengthening the control authority of student publication boards in state colleges, and others advocated organizing the campus newspaper as a controlled formal classroom laboratory. These moves were not adopted very widely because First Amendment guarantees protected the student journalist from state actions.

CHAPTER 2

Independence

Independence is one of the single-value terms in the language. Logically and actually, a person cannot be almost or even a little bit independent. Perhaps independence can be discussed in varying terms in different fields. As for the campus press, independence to be real would have to insist that

1. The publication must be incorporated, but not as a nonprofit educational corporation.
2. The publication cannot receive student fee funds.
3. The publication cannot receive college or university fund allocations, directly or indirectly.
4. The publication cannot use campus facilities or space.
5. The publication cannot enter into any publishing agreements with the university.
6. The publication cannot have a university adviser.
7. The university cannot pay debts or delay bankruptcy of the publication.
8. The university cannot supply technical assistance or advice.
9. The university cannot participate in selection or dismissal of staff members—nor can it take disciplinary action against staff members.
10. The publication cannot have any relationship to any instructional program.
11. No university or college staff person can be on the board of directors of the publication.
12. There can be no stipulations of any kind in the incorporation

charter that in any way relate the publication to the university or college.

13. Membership on the staff of the publication cannot be limited to or specify student status.

14. Readership cannot be confined primarily to students.

15. The name of the publication cannot contain the name of the college or university.

16. The publication cannot be accorded preferential distribution or sales arrangements by the university.

17. There must be no relationship between the publication and the student government.

18. Content of the publication cannot be confined to or dominated by university-related material.

19. No effort, overt or covert, can ever be made by any university person or agency to affect the content of the publication.

20. The university can in no way participate in any legal proceedings involving the publication.

21. The newspaper cannot qualify for a second-class educational mailing permit.

22. The newspaper cannot publish a page of university notices disguised as advertising since such a practice is really subsidization.

23. The newspaper cannot receive mail through the university mail system.

24. The newspaper cannot be licensed or chartered by the university.

25. The university cannot provide placement assistance to newspaper student staff on the basis of learning done on the staff of the publication, nor can it grant course credits for work on the staff not awarded in a similar manner for work on commercial publications. Nor can it require enrollment in university courses.

26. The university cannot specify required grade point averages for student eligibility to be on the staff.

If a student newspaper, yearbook, magazine, or other publication can accurately report that it meets all of these stipulations, it probably can claim to be independent. Could a campus publication meet them? It is possible, but hardly any publication even tries. Perhaps the list seems too demanding, but if "independence" means independence, the points are inescapable. If "independence" does not mean what the list specifies, then independence becomes a myth.

In a College Media Advisers study of the legal status of the student press, a careful evaluation of the reported, repeated, or suggested thinking about being incorporated or being independent was made. Each campus newspaper and yearbook that had any claim of any kind of independence that was real or only figurative was analyzed. Here is a report about many college student publications that believed they were independent of their host institutions.

Some had been incorporated for many years, others only recently. Several were not incorporated at all. By 1972 there were 60 on the list. By 1988 an additional dozen or so publications became incorporated, so the total number now appears to be 80 incorporated, but not necessarily independent, publications in the 3,000 college newspapers in operation. The *Daily Tarheel* of the University of North Carolina incorporated in 1989.

Although the recent move toward this type of independence has been the consequence of conflict, the language of those advocating independence has been couched in Jeffersonian terms intended to obfuscate what is essentially a pragmatic step for the college. Actually, independence would be a financial disaster for the great bulk of campus newspapers or other publications. There is simply not enough advertising available in many campus locales to sustain a quality publication.

The sale of subscriptions would add little to income, if not cut advertising revenue, since the newspaper could deliver only half to a third the readers it did with free circulation or circulation paid for by a student activity fee or by other college allocations.

Even in large communities, newspapers will find it tough going, as the *Daily Californian* at the University of California at Berkeley learned after it became independent under pressure from the regents. The *Californian* discovered it had to run great gobs of advertising to stay in business. "Independence" may give some newspapers the privilege of becoming advertising throwaways.

A study of the campus press sponsored by the American Association of State Colleges and Universities in 1971 might have found new understandings that could have provided more harmonious relationships between the student press and universities. Its basic proposal was to create what it considered an unfinanced incorporated publication, preferably removed physically from the campus. This suggestion has also been made by the American Council on Education.

The prescription for independence would mean reliance on the advertiser, that person who wants to appeal to the mass market. Few student editors conceive of their newspapers as being designed for the "mass audience"; these newspapers are specialty publications for a select audience of college readers. Editors do distinguish between the commercial press and the college press. Student journalists consistently describe their kind of journalism as the "journalism of conscience."

Few critics of the press—collegiate or commercial—would use "dollars and cents" as a criterion for assessing a newspaper's quality. This dollars-and-cents approach leans to a suggestion that campus newspapers be sold rather than distributed freely, because although paid circulation will mean a considerably smaller circulation, facing the test of the marketplace every day, the student editors will usually be forced to turn out a far better paper than if their product relies solely on advertising and is given away daily. However, there is no proof that paid-circulation campus newspapers are any "better" than those distributed free to all on campus. Circulation usually falls off when a newspaper goes from free to paid.

Interviews with student editors would have shown that many oppose reaching only the third to half the students that the paid circulation newspaper goes to. This newspaper is hardly an effective communication force on the campus, they claim.

The most commonly accepted definition of *independence* in describing newspapers refers to news and editorial policy. There are many subsidized campus newspapers that are truly independent in their news and commentary, and there are many "independent" commercial newspapers whose heart, soul, and mind are circumscribed by partisan and/or financial interests.

Since the evidence shows that few campus newspapers can survive the limited advertising marketplace, a question could be asked about just what the purpose of the drive to independence might be. The ostensible reason is that independence removes the institution from responsibility for the student newspaper. The college can always point out that the publication is on its own. But public colleges can do that already by pointing to various federal court decisions that state that the university is not legally the publisher and that it has no content control over campus newspapers. A recommendation that universities "license" these "independent" newspapers hardly seems designed to quiet legislators or regents who understand the First Amendment.

The actual reason for the movement toward independence on the part of some college administrators is to rid the campus of a truly independent critical voice. An examination of court cases involving the student press in public colleges demonstrates that the student press is to be free of the restraints that too many advisers, administrators, presidents, members of governing boards, student government officials, and other persons would place on it through ignorance or design.

Perhaps it is time to recognize that the campus press is different from the commercial press, that it is part of an educational scheme of things, that its very differences should be cherished and cultivated, and that even the commercial press profits from the explorations and experimentations of the campus press.

There are many practical, philosophical, and educational questions that should be explored before the campus press is tossed into the commercial marketplace where it would drift aimlessly and eventually reduce its readers to the same malaise that affects readers of the commercial press. Some of these questions that might be explored are

- What is the nature of subsidy by the educational institution? If physics and sociology instructors, students, and the educational institution itself are subsidized, why not the campus newspaper?
- Does subsidy compromise freedom?
- Is advertising pressure less pernicious than university or student fee funding?
- Should the student press be encouraged to remain an alternative press?

Most appalling of all is the tendency to lump all 3,600 colleges and universities together in one simplistic description and tell administrators everywhere to set up independent, nonfunded student publications.

Here are analyses of reported independent and/or incorporated student publications located by College Media Advisers. The publications proclaimed their independence, but a look at how they operated is instructive. Changes in enrollments, circulations, budgeting, corporate or other structure could well have occurred in these publications and others that could be added. The changes, however, would not appreciably alter the low percentage of independent student publications.

The Agnes Scott College *Profile,* with its 1,100 circulation in 1989, described itself as an independent student newspaper.

At Anchorage Community College of the University of Alaska, a member of the journalism faculty sometimes served as an adviser for the student newspaper, which was owned, operated, and controlled by the students. The student editor served as "publisher."

The University of Arkansas had a plan similar to that of the University of Maryland system.[1] The newspaper received an annual $220,000 allocation at one time, plus free housing, and was under the supervision of a board of publications.[2] In 1986 the allocation had been reduced to $1,000. There were faculty advisers.

Although incorporated and proud of its independence, the student newspaper at Boston College was clearly not independent of student government or the university generally. A member of the journalism faculty served as an adviser. A restructuring of the corporation recently was undertaken to make the newspaper more "responsive" to the students and was "approved" by members of the board of directors of the existing corporation,[3] the president and vice president and members of the congress of the undergraduate government of Boston College, the director of public relations, and the director of student activities. Opinions were to be sought from the president of the college and the student body generally. The yearbook was not incorporated, and a faculty member served as adviser. Circulation of the *Heights* newspapers was 12,000 in 1989.

There were two incorporated independent newspapers in operation at Boston University. The yearbook was not incorporated, it received all of its financing from the university, and members of the staff of the office of student affairs served as advisers.

Student newspapers published on each of the campuses of the University of California were the responsibility of the chancellor on each of the campuses according to an assistant vice president. The newspaper of the Berkeley campus was published by an independent incorporated student cooperative licensed to use the name *Daily Californian* by the board of regents of the university. The student yearbook, however, was not incorporated, was published by the Associated Students, and was not considered to be independent of the university. The *Daily Californian* had a 10-year contract with the university that allowed for the use of the name and also paid a yearly sum of $20,000 for subscriptions for university staff members.

This arrangement evolved after a special four-member commission made up of distinguished American journalists studied the newspaper situation on the university's nine campuses. This commission reported that no ideal "solution" for the problems of the campus press could be proposed.[4] The commission believed the newspapers should have available adequate advising from nonstudents. It suggested that an experienced professional journalist serve as an adviser. It further urged that journalism departments should be ready to provide practical advice to student papers whenever the papers want it.

The commission requested that an autumn professional journalist seminar be held for student editors and that skilled newspaper experts be brought in to discuss reporting, editing, and other journalistic techniques. An important hedge the commission suggested was that each campus produce a newsletter or use other means to circulate official statements. Thus the cost of the total plan could conceivably be greater to each campus than had been the case earlier.

At Berkeley, one of the members of the board of directors of the corporation publishing the newspaper was a professor of journalism at the university.

The contract granted to the *Daily Californian* had several specific provisions.[5] These included

1. The university will not grant a similar license or its privileges to other newspapers or students.

2. The daily publication is to be directed primarily but not exclusively to the students and employees of the Berkeley campus.

3. The *Daily Californian* will publish advertisements submitted to it by the university and will charge the university rates no higher than those charged other advertisers.

4. The *Daily Californian* can never own its name; the university retains all proprietary rights of that name.

5. The *Daily Californian* releases the university for all damages of any kind incurred by the paper.

6. The *Daily Californian* must purchase adequate libel liability insurance, which must cover not only the student members of its staff but also the regents of the University of California.

7. The *Daily Californian* must publish as part of its masthead the following information: "This publication is not an official publication of the University of California, but is published by an independent corporation using the name of the publication as *The Daily Californian* pursuant to a license granted by the Regents of the University of California."

8. The university will pay the papers $20,000 during each academic nine-month year for 2,500 subscriptions.

9. The *Daily Californian* will publish at least 120 issues each academic year.

10. Changes of these provisions must be approved by the University of California.

These 10 provisions indicated that the contract weakened considerably the strength of the supposed independence of the *Daily Californian*. The articles of incorporation further weakened that independence. For example, the license for use of the name enhanced the on-campus distribution possibilities of the newspaper. A question must arise then as to what would happen if the paper were to infuriate the university. The university could cancel its contract and recontract with an alternate newspaper. The threat is clearly possible and could have a severe inhibiting influence on student editors dependent upon a favorable distribution system.

When the articles of incorporation[6] specify that three of the five members of the board of directors must be registered students at the University of California Berkeley campus, the paper does become tied to the university. Further, three-fourths of the staff members also must be University of California registered students.

The *Daily Californian* managed fairly well during its first year of incorporation. Indeed, its 1973 circulation of 31,000 was higher than the enrollment of the Berkeley campus. By 1986, its circulation had dropped to 24,000. Students also had a black newspaper and a university newsletter in 1989.

Comments by Christine E. Weicher, reported by Mel Mencher in an article appearing in the March 1973 issue of *Quill,* raised questions about the success of the venture. She said, "The only merit I see is the freedom we have over our editorial page. Those who have actually benefited from our move off campus are the Regents of the University of California. Independence was never designed to help the newspaper, but rather the Berkeley administrations and the Regents are now safe from possible libel suits and embarrassment." To keep the paper solvent, the paper has become "nothing more than a shopper two of the five days of the week," she indicated.

Mencher further reported, "Independence was suggested to the staff of the *Daily Nexus* on the Santa Barbara campus of the University of California after a conflict with the president. Having watched the sad decline of the *Daily Cal* at Berkeley after it was shoved off the campus by the University, we decided to remain very wary of University motivation, editor Mike Gordan said."[7]

The *Daily Bruin* of the Los Angeles campus of the University of California (UCLA) was not incorporated and received more than $10,000 of student fee funds to provide 24 percent of its budget. Since it had been spicy in content, it was frequently reputed to be independent. It was governed by a board appointed by student government, which frequently attempted to control content and discipline editors. In 1989, there were five other newspapers on campus.

Students of Carroll College in Wisconsin published a student newspaper that had no faculty adviser and was considered independent of the college. However, this evaluation was submitted by a college official serving as chairman of the communications committee. Its 1989 circulation was 1,500.

An independent corporation published the student newspaper and the student yearbook at Colorado College. These publications have had complete freedom throughout the history of the college. The corporation's board of directors included two faculty members, and the paper received student fee funds. Its 1989 circulation was 2,250.

Before World War II, the student newspaper at the University of Colorado was the *Silver and the Gold*. The journalism department maintained an unprinted and unpublished formal laboratory exercise publication called the *Colorado Sun*. The student yearbook was published by the Associated Students and was not considered independent or incorporated. After the war, student activism changed the lot of the newspaper, which became incorporated and changed its name to the *Colorado Daily*.

The articles of incorporation specified that six members of the board of directors had to be students and the seventh member had to be a faculty member of Colorado University.[8] In 1968 the *Daily* ceased receiving student fees. It did have rent-free space provided because the paper was considered an official student organization. One member of the board of regents had labeled the *Daily* system as a "hoax." When the *Daily* ceased receiving student fee money, it had to rely on advertising income. Merchants disliked the paper's radical politics and obscene language. To get more advertising, the paper became far more cautious in language and political positions.[9]

It wasn't long before the *Colorado Daily* wearied of its lot and the university expelled it from campus. The newspaper found a downtown business location from which it has prospered and become a well-directed daily newspaper with circulation on and off campus. It has become a regular commercial newspaper in no way related to the university.

But the university was unable to function well without a student on-campus newspaper. With the help of the journalism department, a semiweekly newspaper with campus relationships was established.

This paper was joined by a weekly publication, so in 1986 Colorado University had its *Campus Press* and its *Collegiate Times*. The university administration also revived the old *Silver and Gold* name to produce a somewhat sentimental faculty house organ.

At the University of Colorado, Denver, an incorporated body, which included the dean of students, a business representative, media representatives, and three students, served as publisher for the independent student newspaper, which was supported by student fees and had a 1989 circulation of 16,000.

The *Spectator*, of Columbia University in New York City, was an incorporated daily with a reported 15,000 circulation in 1986. It had been incorporated since 1961. It had no relationship to the university's graduate school of journalism. The *National Observer,* on January 13, 1973, characterized the *Spectator* as "newly independent."[10] Perhaps the *Observer* was referring to the fact that the university had decided not to allocate student fees to the paper. The *Spectator* has an adviser. The staff borrowed $25,000 from the university to buy typesetting equipment. The *Spectator* could not pay its debt on time; neither could it pay a $16,000 telephone bill to the university. Loans and gifts from alumni kept it alive.

It would be a mistake to assume that the *Spectator* was the only newspaper at Columbia University. For example, the Student Senate of Teachers College produced a newspaper at one time that was financed by university funds. It was ideologically independent of the university, but it was not incorporated. In 1986 university funds provided subsidies to three student magazines and three student newspapers. In 1989 there were at least six student newspapers on the campuses.

The *Cornell Daily Sun* was incorporated and considered itself independent of the university. The university printer, auditor, and legal counsel served as advisers to the staff for the 4,000 circulation newspaper in 1989.

Students published a daily 3,200 circulation newspaper at Dartmouth College. It was incorporated, and its board of directors included faculty members, students, and alumni. In 1989 it had a faculty adviser. A rival conservative newspaper had tormented university administrators for several years.

The *Denver Clarion* of Denver University was a daily with a circulation of 10,000 in 1989. The paper had rent-free housing and an $18,000 yearly allocation from the university, which exercised no controls of its content. The *Clarion* had enjoyed this status and system for many years. Chris Wood, a recent and perceptive editor, dismissed a suggestion of financial independence as providing no benefits that the paper did not have.[11]

The president of Florida State University in Tallahassee decided he could no longer serve as "publisher" of the *Flambeau.* He celebrated his escape by taking away a $92,000 annual student fee allocation. But the *Flambeau* had great difficulty raising enough funds to sustain its operations. It started 1972–73 with a $4,000 deficit. The university decided to help out with free space and facilities, and a $22,000 annual purchase of advertising. This bought a full page four days a week for an official university bulletin page. The copy was furnished by administrative officials.[12] By the 1980s, the *Flambeau* had become a financial success, functioned without university content restraints, and had a circulation of 18,000 in 1989.

A worried University of Florida was instrumental in setting up the *Florida Independent Alligator* as an independent newspaper.[13] The newspaper had been bothersome to the university administration for some time because of its content. The state attorney general, however, ruled that university presidents could neither censor nor be held liable for damaging statements in student newspapers. University presidents had had continual confrontations with faculty, students, and student journalists. One president fired an editor in 1966. In 1969, the American Association of University Professors described the university as repressive. The new president sought to control the newspaper's content. When he discovered he could not do so legally, he imposed "independence."[14]

Students of the university voted 8–1 to keep allocating funds to the newspaper. The imposed independence involved a rental of $217,000 worth of printing equipment and the use of university space and facilities.

Under the Florida plan, the assistant manager of the Campus Shop and Bookstore served as general manager and on the board of directors of the newspaper. The advertising manager was also a member of the board and was a professional journalist. The other four members of the board had served on a commission the president had appointed to revise the plan for operating the newspaper's new corporation. The president did not submit the plan to the University Senate. Members of the Student Senate condemned the president's move and marched on his home the night he announced the plan to deliver a resolution of condemnation since his action "completely ignored the wishes of the student body."[15] By the 1980s, the *Independent Alligator* had solved its financial problems, increased circulation, and believed it was truly independent. Even so, there appears on campus an occasional effort to return it to its former on-campus relationships. The School of Journalism reported in its 1987 *Communigator* that the *Independent Alligator* still has close ties with the university. All editorial staff must be university students. The journalism department chair was on its board. Most of the 13 winners in the Hearst competition were first published in the *Alligator.* Its 1989 circulation was 31,000.

Fontbonne College, in St. Louis, Missouri, reported that it had an independent newspaper that was not incorporated. By 1989 the publication was no longer listed.

The *Harvard Crimson* always appears in articles as the best example of an independent college newspaper. It was a daily with a circulation of 3,500 in 1989, for a university enrollment of 8,862. The *Crimson* and the yearbook were both incorporated, as was a second newspaper published weekly (the *Harvard Independent*). These publications also served Radcliffe College. The *Crimson* had been completely independent of the university since its beginnings. It had been financially strong enough to pay its editor handsomely and to maintain its own building and printing plant off campus.[16] Its board of directors consisted of three alumni who were associated with the paper while students. It used the word *Harvard* as part of its name and had a faculty adviser.

The *Daily Illini,* of the University of Illinois, was an incorporated daily newspaper with a circulation of 11,000 in 1989. It, the yearbook, and a student radio station were considered independent editorially from the university. The charter provisions of the Illini Publishing Company indicated these publications were not truly independent of the university, which has a tradition of incorporating auxiliary agencies. In the provisions stating the purpose of the company, these words clearly place that company as part of the university's operations: "Subject to the general authority of the Chancellor of the University of Illinois, the purpose of this company shall be to publish and distribute student publications."[17]

The corporation had eight members in its board of directors. Four of these were faculty members. The remaining four were students. The board was self-perpetuating since it elected members to fill vacancies. Until a few years ago, the university chancellor appointed the faculty members. Since faculty or student status was required and a full-time publisher was appointed, independence for student journalists was not complete. The board had general supervision of the newspaper, yearbook, and student radio station and established rules and regulations for their control. The corporation purchased a building in 1988 and moved its publications there. The radio station remained in a university building.[18]

The Ithacan Publishing Company, of Ithaca College, a separate corporation independent of the college, published the student newspaper, and Ithacan's publisher was on the newspaper's editorial board. The student yearbook was an official student affairs activity and was not incorporated or considered to be independent of the college. In 1989, the newspaper had a circulation of 4,500.

The Iowa State Daily Publication Board was incorporated and published 16,000 copies of its daily newspaper in 1989. The yearbook was published by its publication board, which was also incorporated. Members of the journalism faculty served as advisers for the newspaper, which was supported in part by student government fees. Two faculty members served as advisers to the yearbook.

Student Publications, Inc., of the University of Iowa, published the newspaper and yearbook. A university official served as publisher. These publications operated independently from an editorial standpoint but were financially dependent on the university. The 1972 edition of the yearbook ended the life of that publication, although efforts to revive it have been made recently. A part-time instructor had served as its adviser. In 1989 the newspaper's circulation was 16,000, and it received a subsidy to cover 30 percent of its costs.

The University Daily Kansas Board at the University of Kansas was incorporated and published the daily newspaper circulating 18,000 copies. The *Jayhawker* yearbook board was also incorporated. Neither the newspaper nor the yearbook was considered independent of the university. Members of the journalism faculty served as advisers for the newspaper staff. The *Daily Kansan* received a 29 percent subsidy from university funds in 1986.

The Kernel Corporation, of the University of Kentucky, was incorporated to publish the daily newspaper, with a 1989 circulation of 17,000. The yearbook was published by a board of student publications and was not considered independent of the university. It received a 50 percent subsidy from university funds in 1986. For a period of time in the 1970s both newspaper and yearbook were troublesome performers; a disillusioned administration was on the verge of discontinuing them both. It hesitated since the half million dollars contributed to the university by the newspaper from its profit established at least a sentimental tie. An energetic adviser and the remarkable young man who served as editor managed to incorporate the newspaper, which eased away from an annual $40,000 student fee allocation to complete dependence on advertising income. A full-time professional advertising director was employed to assure adequate advertising income.

The publisher, who served as general manager and editorial staff adviser, was a university official; 7 of the 13 members of the initial board of directors were college officials.[19] The articles of incorporation require that in the event of its dissolution any remaining assets of the corporation must be transferred to the university to provide journalism scholarships. The newspaper was located in the journalism building, journalism students could earn limited academic credit for working on its staff, and journalism faculty members were available to staff members for pleasant informal advice.

The success of the *Kentucky Kernel* came since it became incorporated, cleaned itself up editorially, purchased typesetting equipment, and stabilized its advertising income to compensate for the withdrawal of student fees. It remained a financial success in 1989.

The students at LaGrange College of Georgia published a newspaper and a yearbook, each of whose editors was considered to serve as publisher. The publications were considered independent of the college. No faculty advisers were provided. Neither publication was incorporated. The newspaper received 50 percent of its income from student fees in 1986 and had a 1989 circulation of 750.

Apparently the student editors for the newspaper and the yearbook at the Los Angeles College of Optometry in the 1970s were publishers of the publications, which were considered independent of the college, which provided no faculty advisers. The publications were not incorporated.

Student editors of the newspaper and the yearbook at the University of Southern Maine campus at Portland and Gorham served as publishers for the publications, considered independent of the university, which provided no faculty advisers. The publications were not incorporated. The *Free-Press* had a 1989 circulation of 4,500.

Maryland Media, Inc., at the University of Maryland, published the student daily newspaper, a black biweekly newspaper, a magazine, and a yearbook that received $40,000 subsidy in 1986. The *Diamondback* had a 1989 circulation of 21,000. (The *Hakoach* was a newspaper for Jewish students.) Two university faculty members were on its board of directors, by charter provisions. It used rent-free university space. The publications, although edited independently and published by an independent publisher, were and must remain a part of the university community according to the board of regents.[20]

Recently the editor of the *Diamondback* discovered that his newspaper really wasn't independent, although it had been proclaimed to be in earlier days. University officials found he had not enrolled in any classes; they sent him an edict to enroll or resign. He enrolled to keep his job.

No agency or person served as publisher of the student publications at Marymount Manhattan College (New York), which considered them independent of the college.[21] The publications were not incorporated.

The *Michigan State News,* of Michigan State University, was an incorporated daily newspaper with a 1989 circulation of 37,000. A university official served as publisher. The *Wolverine* yearbook was a university publication whose publisher, a faculty member, approved its content prior to publication. Content of the newspaper did not undergo prior approval since it was independent of the university in content.

Article 6 of the *Academic Freedom Report for Students* at Michigan State University defined *student publications* as publications in which students have been involved in writing, publishing, and distributing, and included publications of student living units, governing groups, student organizations, and other student groups. Students were assured maximum freedom of expression and ideas in such publications. Administrative units could also authorize funds for and assume sponsorship of publications germane to the administrative unit. Control of content and editorial policy were guaranteed to all such publications, subject only to the advice and counsel of the administrator or administrative unit. Circulation and subscription sales were rigidly regulated.[22]

The *Michigan Daily* produced 15,000 copies in 1989 for students at the University of Michigan. It and the yearbook were published by the Board for Student Publications, which included faculty members. In the Code of Ethics of the *Daily,* which every staff member was admonished to read and understand, the "independence" of the paper becomes quite clear. The preamble stated, "As a newspaper published by the University of Michigan it is incumbent upon the *Daily* always to have at heart the interests of the University, and to refrain from any such actions as may compromise the University in the eyes of the Legislature." The code for the *Michigan Daily* prescribed:[23]

1. The editorial page shall not reflect one point of view to the exclusion of all others.

2. Editorials badly written, in poor taste, or based on faulty thinking will be denied publication.

3. Racial or religious bias cannot be in editorials.

4. Political discussion shall be confined specifically to issues and shall never embrace personal attacks on political figures.

5. The *Daily* will not take sides in elections to the Board of Regents.

6. There shall be no discussion of state appropriations to the University without previous editorial consultation with the members of the Board in Control of Student Publications.

7. Members of the staff are to seek advice and assistance from faculty members throughout the campus.

8. All interviews with faculty members shall be checked with the interviewee either personally or by phone before they are published.

9. Reports of University lectures shall, whenever possible, be checked with the head of the department sponsoring the particular lecture.

10. Sex crimes shall not be discussed in news or editorial columns.

11. Violent crimes, except of immediate local interest, shall not be discussed.

12. Suicides of alumni shall not be reported, except if they occur in the immediate vicinity, in which case they shall be dealt with extreme care.

13. Crimes involving students or faculty shall not be reported without first notifying University authorities.
14. News items of a pornographic nature shall have no place in the *Daily*.

In a practical sense, student staff members generally ignored these prohibitions, written in 1940, because they are journalistically ludicrous. The vice president for university relations reported that the public did not consider the *Daily* as being independent of the university.[24]

Despite the above data, the *Michigan Daily* is frequently pointed to as an example of an "independent" newspaper. The newspaper had been strong financially. Its building was paid for from yearbook and newspaper profits and it paid for its utilities. Even so, it frequently had a sizable profit each year; however, it fell on bad times financially in the 1980s.

New York University in New York City is a private university composed of several schools and colleges. The Washington Square Center had five publications in 1989 that were in the newspaper category. The *Washington Square News* was the regular news, features, and sports newspaper, with a circulation of 18,000. The administration of the university considered the editorial boards of the newspapers to be agencies publishing them. The papers used phrases like "published by the students of New York University." The *Washington Square News* received 25 percent of its operating budget from a university subsidy.

The Observer, of the University of Notre Dame in Indiana, established in 1966, considered itself an independent newspaper serving Notre Dame and St. Mary's College, with a 1989 circulation of 12,000.

The *Campus Echo,* of North Carolina Central University, had its university funds taken away. It became defunct, but a recent court decision restored that funding.[25] By 1989 its circulation reached 5,500.

All campus communications media of Northland College in Wisconsin were under the total control of the Northland College Communications Commission, Inc. These included the student newspaper, the yearbook, a literary magazine, and a radio station. This incorporation was considered strong enough to make the publications "absolutely, legally, and actually 'independent' of the College." But members of the faculty served as advisers on an informal basis. A description of the commission raised questions about "independent."[26] The 1989 newspaper circulation was 800.

The Communications Commission was composed of nine members: three students, selected by the Student Association; four student editors; one faculty member; and one administrator. If there was a dispute on the commission, a student supreme court settled it. The Communications Commission had an independent budget, and the college served as collection agency. There was no way the college or the Student Association could censor any campus media, and the Communications Commission was prohibited from doing so by its bylaws.

The commission appointed the four editors. Each editor appointed a staff, which had to be made up of students, and the commission confirmed these appointments. Among the reasons the commission could use to dismiss an editor were these: (1) Publication of slanderous, libelous, or defamatory statements, or the broadcast thereof, as defined by the Northland College Criminal Code, though no prosecution under the criminal code need occur. (2) The publication or broadcasting of demonstrably false or misleading statements designed to cause panic or damage to persons or property. The bylaws of the commission clearly indicated that Northland College did not really comprehend the nature of libel.

The Student Publishing Company, Inc., of Northwestern University published the yearbook and the daily newspaper, which circulated 8,500 copies in 1989. A faculty member served as chair of the Board of Student Publications, which was also the board of directors of the corporation and included three faculty members and one alumnus, all appointed by the university president, and three students elected by the Student Senate. The president-treasurer of the board was required to make an annual report to the president of the university and other reports required by university rules and regulations. The board selected editors and business managers for the publications and could dismiss them for cause. The board determined salaries paid student staff members.[27] The constitution and bylaws of the Student Publishing Company, Inc., had to be approved by the Student Senate.

The O'Collegian Publishing Company, Inc., of Oklahoma State University, published a daily newspaper with 12,000 circulation in 1989. The board of directors of Student Publications published the yearbook. Neither the yearbook nor the newspaper was considered independent of the university. Journalism faculty members served as advisers, and the director of the School of Journalism was publisher. Five university officials and the student newspaper editor were the six members of the board of directors of the O'Collegian Publishing Company.[28]

The Emerald Publishing Company, Inc., of the University of Oregon, published 11,000 copies in 1989. The board of directors included three faculty members appointed by the president and three students appointed by the student body president, as well as the editor and the business manager of the paper.[29] Each year the corporation had to negotiate with the student government for bulk subscriptions of about $26,400, and $7,500 worth of bulk subscriptions had to be contracted with the university administration.

The *Daily Emerald* was frequently cited as an example of an independent newspaper, but it obviously was dependent on annual subscription negotiations and a board dominated by representatives of student government and university administration. In 1986, the student government sponsored its own publication, the *Record.* The *Beacon* also rivaled the *Emerald.*

The Collegian, Inc., of Pennsylvania State University, published 19,200 copies of a daily newspaper for the university in 1986. The yearbook was a chartered student organization and was not considered independent. As a matter of fact, an administrative official had approved yearbook content prior to publication throughout the 1970s. The newspaper had no official tie, yet it was provided office space, and the university bought subscriptions for free distribution. It did not have to obtain a student organization charter to function. Students and faculty were members of the corporation's board.

The Daily Princetonian Publishing Company, Inc., at Princeton University, published 3,300 copies of a daily newspaper in 1989 for the university's students. The yearbook was sponsored by the junior and senior classes. The Princeton tradition of a free press for students dated back to the eighteenth century. A faculty member was on the board of directors. It uses the word *Princeton* in its name.

The *Exponent,* of Purdue University, is frequently cited as an example of an independent newspaper. This view grew out of a clash with the administration that was badly handled by those officials. The *Exponent,* which has a strong tradition, has had its good years and bad ones. Financially it has done so well that its circulation increased to about 19,000 in the 1980s. In 1989, it constructed its own building off campus so it could escape the dingy basement of the Student Union. It has undergone periods of severe criticism for content by university officials. Editors of the *Exponent* became embroiled in a squabble several years ago about the improper operation of the student government election commission. The Student Senate voted "no confidence" in the editors and went to the publishing board with a request that the editors be fired. The board turned down the Student Senate, but it could have fired the editors.

The *Exponent* escaped student government interference by incorporation. The articles of incorporation provide for freedom of the press for the newspaper student staff, even though a publisher served as general manager of the operation.

The *Phoenix* newspaper, of Queens College of CUNY, was published by Student Press, Inc. *Newsbeat* was published by a club chartered by the college. Both were considered independent of the university; however, faculty members and administrators were members of the board of directors. In 1989 *Newsbeat*'s circulation was 19,000 and *Phoenix*'s was 10,000. Four other newspapers were published at Queens.

The student newspaper at Saint Leo College in Florida was considered to be independent of the college to a great extent, as was the yearbook. Both publications are financed 100 percent by subsidies. The *Monarch* newspaper had a 1989 circulation of 1,500.

The student newspaper of Saint Mary's College in Indiana operated independently of the college, but the yearbook had advisers, one of whom approved copy prior to publication.

The student newspaper of Salisbury State College in Maryland had been involved in the process of incorporating, but it was not clear that the effort survived until the 1980s, when its circulation was 3,800.

The campus newspaper and yearbook at the University of South Dakota were published by an incorporated Student Publications Board. The bylaws of this board indicated that the principal office of the publications shall be the university. The board members included two students appointed by the student association president and approved by the head of the journalism division, and one appointed by the public relations office. A journalism faculty member was an ex-officio member of the board who also served as adviser for the newspaper and yearbook. The 1989 circulation of the newspaper was 6,000.

Student publications could be assigned to the board's jurisdiction by the student association president and by university officials who were sponsors of such publications. The board appointed and dismissed and established salaries. It was financially and legally responsible for editorial content and financial transactions.[30]

Although the newspaper at San Francisco State College was incorporated, it was not independent of the university. The Associated Students published the paper and provided 5 percent of operating costs from student fees. In 1989 circulation was 15,000. The Journalism Department also published a newspaper in laboratory classes.

The *Stanford Daily*, of Stanford University, with a circulation of 15,000 in 1989, has received considerable attention as an independent newspaper. Its corporation was operated by a nine-member board, five of whom were students. Student fee funds and university bulk subscriptions were phased out over a three-year period. The university provided housing at a nominal rental since it had a building constructed from funds specifically given to the university for housing student publications. The *Daily* received 10 percent of its budget in subsidy. Stanford had four other newspapers.

The newspaper and yearbook at the State University of New York, Stonybrook, was considered independent in 1972. The newspaper was published by the Statesman Association, which was not incorporated. In 1987 the newspaper circulation was 12,000, and it received 50 percent of its budget in subsidy. By 1989 a second newspaper, the *Stoney Brook Press,* with its 10,000 copies, was 80 percent financed by student fees.

The Board of Student Publications at Southern Methodist University had published the student newspaper for many years, but a Student Publishing Company became incorporated. The director of student publications and faculty advisers worked with the staffs of the publications. The student government sought in 1988 to regulate the 5,000 circulation newspaper's content and circulation practices. A weekly newspaper was also published.

The *Daily Beacon* of the Knoxville campus of the University of Tennessee tried "independence" for a while, but it went so badly in debt that the university had to reinstall it as a university activity and pay off its debts. It reached a circulation of 16,000 in 1989.

Publications at the Chattanooga campus were not considered independent and had faculty advisers.

The newspaper and yearbook at Vassar College were both considered to be independent of the College. This plan was not a new one at Vassar since the publications had always been independent. They were published by the staff and were not incorporated. The *Miscellany News* had a 1989 circulation of 3,300, financed partly by an 80 percent subsidy. A consumer advocacy paper established in 1976, *Unscrewed,* had a 3,500 circulation in 1986 and was financed with a 100 percent subsidy. *Vassar Views* was financed by a 100 percent subsidy.

The board of visitors of the University of Virginia was considered the publisher of the newspaper—an incorporated daily with a 14,000 circulation in 1989. The yearbook was incorporated and appeared to be more independent of the university than the newspaper. There was a second newspaper with 10,000 copies each week.

Campus Publications, Inc., at Washington University in St. Louis, published the newspaper. It was considered independent of the university, which provided a publications adviser from the student affairs area. An accounting professor was president of the corporation, whose board included four faculty members appointed by the Faculty Senate Council, two administrators appointed by the chancellor from among student affairs officials and from the university publications office, two student appointed by the Student Union, and two students from publications staffs.[31] The newspaper had a 1989 circulation of 18,000 and received 24 percent of its budget from subsidies and mandatory fees.

The Student Government Association of Western Illinois State University contracted with a private incorporated publisher to produce a newspaper. The staff was hired by that publisher, who used students and nonstudents as paid employees. The Student Government Association published a yearbook whose staff was advised about content prior to publication by a director of publications. The newspaper system was an attempt to sidestep an Illinois legal provision that declared each Illinois state college or university the publisher of student publications organized with institutional sponsorship, supported in whole or part with state funds originating from student activity funds. Each institution was directed to promulgate policies for sustaining publications of high quality.

Institutional leadership was responsible for student publications in accord with the objectives of the institutions. The Board of Governors of State Colleges and Universities endorsed the principle of freedom of expression and recognized the obligations, legal and ethical, common to all publications of high quality. The truth and judgment implicit in responsible communications were expected to be observed in assessing whether material for student publications satisfied such obligations.[32] This system broke down, and the newspaper was returned to the campus at Western Illinois. The newspaper had a 1989 circulation of 6,000 and received funding from student fees. The yearbook received an 80 percent subsidy.

The student newspaper and yearbook of William Paterson College in New Jersey were both considered independent of the college. The newspaper was incorporated and had a 1989 circulation of 10,000. The yearbook received 80 percent of its income from student activity fees. Faculty advisers were provided.

At Roger Williams College in Rhode Island the newspaper was published by Student Publications, Inc., and the yearbook was published by student government. A faculty adviser approved yearbook content prior to publication, and it was considered independent of the college, as the newspaper was. The board of directors was made up of students, and the paper received 30 percent of its 1986 budget from mandatory fees, with a 1989 circulation of 3,000.

The newspaper at the University of Wisconsin at Green Bay was considered to be incorporated. It was supported by student fees. The newspaper was covered by the 1965 statement of the board of regents of the University of Wisconsin, which encouraged and supported freedom of expression in student publications. Its 1989 circulation was 3,200.

The *Daily Cardinal,* at the University of Wisconsin at Madison, published 15,000 copies in 1989. Both newspaper and yearbook were incorporated. Although considered independent of the university, both must be controlled by students. The board of regents encouraged and supported freedom of expression in student publications. The board believed that no regent, legislator, or other person should be able to prescribe what shall be orthodox and therefore acceptable for publication and what shall be unorthodox and therefore interdicted.[33] There was also a weekly newspaper.

Sophomores elected two juniors and another member of the board of the *Wisconsin Badger* yearbook corporation. Each board member stayed in office until the end of his or her senior year. Three faculty members appointed by the president served as advisory members of the board.[34]

Five members of the board of the *Cardinal* daily newspaper must be students, elected by students in campuswide voting. Three faculty members were appointed by the president of the university.

The Student Life and Interests Committee of the University of Wisconsin had the same jurisdiction over the Daily Cardinal Corporation that it had over other student organizations, except that it had no voice in matters of editorial or business policy or in the selection or retention of personnel (except as to eligibility) of the *Daily Cardinal.*[35]

The *Yale Daily News* circulated 5,000 copies in 1989. It is cited often as an independent newspaper. Its board of directors included student staff members and alumni who served as staff members while students. It used *Yale* in its name.

Additional incorporated publications included the *Bradley Scout* of Bradley University, the *Pine Burr* of Campbell College, the *Rocky Mountain Collegian* of Colorado State University, the *Courtbouillon* of Dillard University, the *Fountainhead* of East Carolina University, the *Red and Black* of Georgia University, the *Communicator* of Indiana University-Purdue University at Fort Wayne, the *Collegian* of Kansas State University, the *Daily* of the University of Minnesota, the *Oakland Sail* of Oakland University, the *Daily Barometer* of Oregon State University, the *Collegian* of the University of Richmond, the *Quill* of Roger Williams University, the *Spartan Daily* of San Jose State University, the *Digest* of Southern University, the *Daily Orange* of Syracuse University, The *Daily* of Washington University, and the *Port* of the University of Wisconsin at Milwaukee.

Although proud of their corporations and editorial freedoms, these publications do not make an issue of being independent of their colleges or universities. Careful reading of the data from each of the colleges indicates that student publications have great difficulty measuring up to the 26 criteria of an independent publication. The *Harvard Crimson* and the *Yale Daily News* may come closest. Each of these newspapers has an alumni board of directors in its corporation and uses the name of its university in the newspaper name. Several of the larger incorporated and unincorporated newspapers, especially dailies, have experienced excellent financial achievements during the late 1980s.

From studies it becomes clear that incorporation alone does not mean or assure editorial independence for editors. Nor does independence require incorporation; many of the publications considered to be independent were not incorporated. Perhaps the term *independence* is somewhat misleading since many relationships do and will exist between student publications and host institutions. Actually, the ideal situation in both public and private colleges is the establishment and maintenance of an atmosphere of freedom of expression for student publications. If the editors can publish without prior restraint or fear of subsequent institutional punishment, an ideal situation exists, and it can exist under several structural plans. The sincerity of many college officials in seeking to achieve this ideal has led to discussions, some incorporations, and strong achievements and learning by student journalists.

Information gathered by College Media Advisers in the 1970s and early 1980s presents overwhelming data based on 1,452 publications in 898 colleges and universities. It demonstrates that in fact and preference, America's institutions of higher education have not rushed, trended, or even limped to an incorporated college student press. Data also may be found in the 1989 *College Media Directory,* which indicated there might be 107 independent publications.[36]

Lillian Lodge Kopenhaver, of Florida International University and a former president of College Media Advisers, and Ron Spielberger, of Memphis State University and headquarters manager for College Media Advisers, conducted a study of the 1988 and 1989 status of the "independent" college student press.[37] Their report follows.

> The independence of college and University student newspapers is a topic that has been often debated, with as many definitions of independence emerging as there are collegiate newspapers.
>
> [26 criteria for independence at the beginning of this chapter] have often been looked to for guidance by advisers and student editors as they

work to set up their own operations free from administrative and/or other interference. Yet many newspapers which are self-defined as independent deviate from these guidelines. To what extent are "independent" newspapers really independent? What does independence as staff and advisers define it today really mean? Just how do they define it?

Methodology

This study was initiated as part of the effort of College Media Advisers to provide information on college media operations nationally. In the fall of 1988, College Media Advisers surveyed the 797 college and University newspapers listed in the 1987 Editor and Publisher Yearbook to ascertain how the independence of student newspapers is perceived throughout the country and how truly independent student newspapers are. Of the 797 questionnaires mailed out, 34.5% (275) of the individuals surveyed responded to the 17 questions.

Results

More than half the respondents (53.8% or 148) represent four-year colleges and universities; 26.8% (n = 148) are at four-year private institutions and 18.8% (n = 51) at two-year public colleges. Three respondents did not list their affiliations. There were no returns from two-year private colleges.

More than half the institutions (58.2% or 160) report having independent student newspapers. Of those, more than half (54.4% or 87) are at four-year public colleges and universities, 26.3% (n = 42) at four-year private schools and 19.3% (n = 31) at two-year public colleges.

Publications Boards

More than two-thirds of the schools (68.3% or 183) have publications boards. Of four-year public institutions, more than three-fourths (79.5% or 116) have such boards; in addition, 62.5% (n = 45) of four-year private schools and 44% (n = 22) of two-year public colleges also have publications boards. Of independent newspapers, nearly two-thirds (60.8% or 107) have boards.

Nearly three-fourths of respondents (72.3% or 149) indicate that the publications board selects the newspaper editor. Of independent student newspapers, nearly two-thirds (62.1% or 87) report that publications boards select the editor. Of these schools with publications boards, more than three-fourths (79.7% or 145) select the editor.

Nearly one-third of colleges and universities (31.6% or 54) indicate that their publications boards report to the president of the institution, more than any other single source; 11.1% (n = 19) report to student governments, 8.8% each (n = 15) to the chairman of the journalism department/school and to the student affairs vice president/dean, 6.4% (n = 11) to the adviser, 4.6% (n = 8) each to the board of regents and the faculty senate and 2.9% (n = 5) to the newspaper staff. Ten publications (5.8%)

indicate that the board reported to no one; it was responsible to itself. These percentages are the same in all categories for independent student newspapers and very similar for college and universities with publications boards.

Adviser/General Manager/Publisher

Colleges and universities report that the chairman of the journalism/communications department or school hires the adviser, general manager or publisher of the newspaper in more instances than any other (31.5% or 74).

The newspaper staff follows with 14.5% (n = 34); the student affairs administration names the manager in 12.8% (n = 30) of the cases, the publications board also in 12.8% (n = 30) and the president of the institution in 9.8% (n = 23). Nearly one-quarter of the schools (18.2% or 43) list other sources which include the board of trustees, the vice president/dean of academic affairs and the vice president of university affairs. Several publications indicate that they have no adviser/general manager, but are independent corporations run by the board of directors of the corporation; a number of other newspapers respond that the adviser/general manager/publisher is a volunteer.

In the cases of independent newspapers, the pattern is quite similar; nearly one-third (27.7% or 38) being hired by the department or school chairman, 16.8% (n = 23) by the newspaper staff, 10.2% (n = 14) by the student affairs administration, 12.4% (n = 17) by the publications board, and 9.5% (n = 13) by the president.

More than half the schools responding (52.7% or 145) report that the adviser, general manager or publisher is paid totally from university funds; most respondents note that this is part of a faculty teaching load. A smaller number, (9.8% or 27) are paid totally from student activities fees and 9.5% (n = 26) from advertising revenue.

Nearly one-fifth, (19.6% or 54) are paid partially from several sources, most frequently a combination of the communications unit and advertising revenue, or between the communications unit and student affairs.

Of those newspapers reporting their status as independent, 53.7% (n = 87) of the advisers, managers or publishers are paid totally from university funds, 12.3% (n = 20) from advertising revenue, 10.5% (n = 17) from student activity fees. Nearly one-fifth (18.5% or 30) are paid from several sources.

Finances

Nearly two-thirds of the newspapers responding (64% or 165) rely upon the university's accounting office to write checks for their bills; 24% (n = 62) use their own accounting department. Of independent newspapers, almost the same pecentages apply; 58.8% (n = 90) rely upon the university for accounting services and 27.4% (n = 42) use their own accountants.

Excess revenues from the newspaper operation remain with the publication in nearly two-thirds (69.7% or 180) of the cases responding; 14.5% (n = 38) report profits going into a university fund and 8.8% (n = 23) into the student activity fund. Of independent newspapers, a higher percentage (73.5% or 114) keep excess revenue; 10.3% (n = 16) report revenues going into university funds and 8.4% (n = 13) into student activity funds.

If the newspaper does not generate enough advertising or other revenue to meet expenses, two-thirds of the respondents report that either the university (33.9% or 84) or the newspaper itself (33.5% or 83) would be responsible for those excess expenses. Nearly one-fourth (27.4% or 68) report other alternatives, including the student government (n = 30) paying and the debt being carried forward to the next year (n = 10); only 5.2% (n = 13) placed responsibility with the journalism or communication department or school.

In the case of independent newspapers, the figures are quite similar; 36.8% (n = 53) place responsibility with the publication itself; 31.3% (n = 45) with the university and 25.7% (n = 27) with other sources including the student government association and the next year's budget. Only 6.2 (n = 9) report reliance on the communication unit.

Approval of advertising rates, budget, and major equipment purchases for the newspaper resides with the adviser, publisher, or general manager in nearly one-half of the newspaper operations (44.2% or 99); at nearly one-fifth (18.8% or 42) the responsibility resides with the publications board and a few (5.8% or 13 each) give the student affairs and communications unit the responsibility. One-fourth (25.4% or 57) list other areas, including the editorial board or the student business manager (n = 17) and the student government association (n = 10). Eleven newspapers state that the board of directors of the corporation is given that responsibility. On newspapers listed as independent, the figures are almost identical.

Most of the newspapers (86.6% or 232) do not pay their own utility bills or pay rent for space (89.7% or 244); of independent papers, 83.5% (n = 132) do not pay utility bills and 87% (n = 140) do not pay rent.

Nearly all (90.7% or 245) do their own advertising billing; the same is true for independent newspapers (91.8% or 146). Most papers (79.2% or 210) control their own advertising revenue accounts; a slightly higher percentage (81.5% or 128) of independent newspapers report the same.

Nearly three-fourths of campus newspapers (69.8% or 192) generate 50% or more of their revenue from advertising; 25 newspapers (9%) are totally self-sufficient from advertising. With regard to student activity fees, more than one-fourth (27.6% or 76) generate 50% or more of their revenue from this source; 7 papers (2.5%) receive 100% of their revenue from these fees.

Slightly more than one-fourth (28% or 67) receive university allocations; 14.5% (n = 40) receive 50% or more and 5.8% (n = 16) receive 100%
from the university.

Less than one-fourth (24% or 66) of the newspapers sell subscriptions; all generate between 1 and 50% of their revenue from this source.

Independent newspapers have virtually the same percentages as all
newspapers reporting, with only 10.5%, or 17 newspapers, receiving their
total substinence from advertising.

What is Independent?

[This study] stresses the fact that in order to be truly independent, a
student newspaper—or any other student medium, for that matter—must
have no formal ties to its college or university. More than half the student
newspapers responding to this study stated they were independent.

Yet, only two-thirds of them have publications boards, only 11.1%
of those boards hire the adviser, manager or publisher from non-university funds—advertising revenues. In addition, only slightly more than
one-fourth of independent papers use their own accounts to write checks
for bills; only one-third assume responsibility for debts incurred at year
end and 9.2% do not do their own advertising billing.

Only 16.5% pay their utility bills and 13% pay rent. Slightly more
than one-fourth place approval of advertising rates, budget and major
equipment purchase with sources other than the adviser, publisher or general manager, the publications board, or the board of directors of the
corporation.

Finally, only 10%, or 17 newspapers, generate their total income from
advertising revenues.

Several publications stress the total independence of their newspaper:
10 publications, 5.8%, indicate that their publications boards report to no
one, but are responsible to themselves; 11 newspapers state that they are
independent corporations without an adviser, general manager or
publisher and are run by their board of directors.

One large northwestern university daily reports that it is a "nonprofit,
tax-paying domestic corporation, totally independent from the university."
The publisher is a 10-member board of directors which acts in matters of
finance, policy, and personnel. The board is composed of three elected
staff members from the associated students, two at-large positions to be
elected through application (student, faculty, staff or community), one
faculty and one staff appointed by the administration, and one commu-
nity-at-large member selected by the board.

Revenue at the daily is generated from advertising and subscriptions.
A bulk subscription is sold to students and to faculty and staff. Space is
leased; all telephone bills, supplies, and equipment are paid for and payroll
and taxes are paid. The board determines the ad ratio of the paper and the
editor "has total autonomy with regard to editorial content."

With regard to personnel, the board is "responsible for hiring and termination of department head personnel, reviewing performances and negotiating personnel contracts"; with regard to finances, the board oversees financial and budgetary decisions "with fiscal responsibilities to the perpetuation" of the daily and examines and reviews "the purchases of major capital acquisitions of equipment, furnishings, and land"; and with regard to policy, the board insures that the corporation "is adhering to accepted practices and policies of the publishing media" as stated in the articles of incorporation.

This model was closely echoed by two northeastern dailies.

One southeastern university daily offers slight variations on this model, with a general manager hired, along with the editor and managing editor, by the board of directors, which acts as publisher, reports only to itself, and selects its own members. The newspaper is located off campus in non-university space and pays full market-value rent; it has absolutely no contractual or even informal guarantees from the university. Funding is generated totally from advertising revenues.

Conclusions

Statistics indicate that very few student newspapers are truly independent. Perhaps 5% of the nation's student papers fall into the independent category, as defined by [this study's] indicators and by common denominators in the business. In order to achieve editorial and financial independence and to insure that legal liability resides with the publication, all ties to the college or university must be conducted as a separate business, with the publication assuming full responsibility for all expenses it accrues or services it uses and for generating all revenues it receives. Those factors indicate real independence.

Any other status—from the adviser/general manager/publisher being paid partially by student activity or university funds or being responsible to a university official—to university accounting services being used—to funding for the operation being received from student activity or university funds—is partial independence by any definition.

Student newspapers must assess the degree to which real independence is desirable and necessary to their operations and to their readership; this may indicate that some of the factors which make them partially independent must be readjusted. Total independence means accepting ultimate responsibility for all parts of the publication operation.

The true measure of being an independent editorial voice and exercising the constitutional right of a free press resides in the ability of a college publication to publish its views of the college world and the larger world in its own way and words without prior restraint or subsequent punishment. Both public and private colleges should cherish, nurture, and provide in policies and practices for such an atmosphere and reality on their campuses.

CHAPTER 3

Funding

Money is tight on the campus. Budgets are being squeezed by the pressures of inflation, the need to modernize facilities and curriculums, and the market's dictates for higher faculty salaries. Dwindling enrollments hurt, but increasing enrollment in the late 1980s hurt even more. An antiintellectualism is selling the belief that one or two years of technical or vocational post–high school study is the ultimate for most young people in contemporary society. Bruises are healing well from the days of violent campus demonstrations, but the memory is still a frightening specter. The anti–South Africa demonstrations against apartheid and other political issues might rekindle campus militancy. And the underground press, with its romantically incorrect name, has simply run out of steam for the time being.

College administrators and board members look at shrinking funds, piled in smaller budget piles. They take a bit from here and there to meet the crises and urgencies every month brings.

They remember the attacks made on the campus standard press and begin to attach credulity to them. Some believe students really don't want a campus newspaper, yearbook, or magazine. This is an astonishing conclusion, especially from a college president who makes speeches about the need for communications on the campus, in the nation, and around the world.

But budget makers say take some or all of the money away from the student publications, which aren't very important or very popular, and always carry an implied threat anyhow. That money can be used better elsewhere.

When a thesis comes along that says a student newspaper that receives student fee money can never be as independent as one cut off from the university without a dime, the fee raiders hurrah and produce rationales with grand phrases to excuse their depletion.

Perhaps this section of this report should weep for the student publications thus impoverished, but it is really concerned about the college that believes it is going to save or make money by dumping the student publications.

Things just don't work out that way!

Here is what is more apt to happen.

Thomas Fischer caught the point. He tells us, "In these days of increasing student press independence it may prove advisable or necessary for an institution to establish its own house organ to communicate accurately and punctually information concerning its news, schedules, policies, etc."[1] Such a house organ costs money to produce. Printing it wouldn't be cheaper than printing the student newspaper unless fewer issues with fewer pages and less communications functions were produced. And the professional staff members doing the work would command higher salaries than the student staff could receive. Fischer solves the money problem neatly: "Student fee monies can be provided" (for these official nonstudent publications).[2]

There have been such publications as the Columbia University *Newsletter,* the Harvard University *Gazette,* the Stanford *Observer,* and others. Students in many cases simply ignore these promotional house organs. Communication happens only when a reader reads, not because an administrator wishes.

Another problem arises when the student newspaper has its funds taken away and is pushed from the university. Some 300 institutions maintain a journalism instructional program. Journalism students report, write, edit, publish, and catch hell for whatever they did wrong from a vocal and perceptive audience of peers called students and faculty. The campus press provides a lively laboratory for these students. Some colleges organize this experience very formally, some quite loosely. In some colleges, pressure from student factions have forced a splitting away from the journalism faculty by the student newspapers. In others, the journalism faculty has fled the campus press, either from fear of involvement or to find more pleasant avenues of academe to travel. But something happens. The journalism faculty discovers they need a laboratory newspaper or publication, so in come the requests for funds to sustain such a learning laboratory. This costs money!

An additional problem can arise. The supposedly independent student newspaper simply cannot manage financially. For example, take the case of the *Spectator* of Columbia University. Student fee allocations ended. But the university loaned the paper $25,000 for cold-type equipment. When the paper couldn't pay the loan, the university authorized an additional $20,000 grant but found the paper owed $16,470 for telephone bills. So the phone bill, the grant, and the debt made a blockbuster headache for everyone. An independent paper does not necessarily relieve the university of money problems. The *Spectator* did solve its financial problems finally.

North Carolina presents an interesting case. Four students sued the university at Chapel Hill, challenging the use of mandatory student fees to support the student newspaper, the *Daily Tarheel.* This suit followed an episode at North Carolina Central University, which had been mandated to withhold funds from the paper by a state court because some students had objected to its contents. The *Campus Echo,* cut off from student fee funds, simply could not operate. So the students of the college had no paper.

When the case of the *Campus Echo* came to the U.S. court of appeals, here is what happened: The president of a state university, who withdrew financial support to the campus newspaper because of its editorial policy, abridged the freedom of the press in violation of the First and Fourteenth Amendments, the federal appellate court in Richmond ruled. Student fees had been used to support publication of the official campus newspaper. However, editorial comments advocated racial segregation and objected frequently to the school's policy of admitting an increasing number of white students. The federal district court in North Carolina ruled there was no violation of the First and Fourteenth Amendments in cutting off financial support but also ruled that the school should permit the publication to continue to be published and distributed on the campus.

On appeal, the appellate court said the censorship of student publications at state-supported institutions cannot be imposed "by suspending the editors, suppressing circulation, requiring imprimaturs of controversial articles, excising repugnant material, withdrawing financial support, or asserting any other form of censorial oversight based on the institution's power of the purse." The appeals court did note that students, like others, are forbidden to incite or produce imminent lawless action. "The record contains no proof that the editorial policy of the paper incited harassment, violence, or interference with white students and faculty. At the most, the editorial comments advocated racial segregation contrary to the Fourteenth Amendment and the Civil Rights Act of 1964," the court added. Also, there was no indication that the paper refused to allow the expression of contrary views.

Another issue in the case was whether there was racial discrimination in the staffing of the newspaper and accepting advertising. The equal protection clause forbids racial discrimination in extracurricular activities of a state-supported institution, the court said, and freedom of the press furnishes no shield for discrimination in advertising.

The case was remanded to district court so that the university president could amend his pleadings to apply for relief against discriminatory practices in staffing and advertising. The appeals court indicated, nevertheless, that the permanent withdrawal of funds was not an appropriate remedy.[3]

Actually there is no legal, philosophical, or practical reason not to allocate student fee monies to the campus press. Failure to do so leads to financial problems for both the university and the publication. Use of student fee money for a well-written, well-edited, reasonable, and intelligent campus newspaper is a positive way to provide for freedom of expression and effective communications in an ongoing and stable manner. This is educational achievement.

By 1985 courts had considered 20 cases challenging the legal authority for state colleges to use mandatory student fees to finance student publications. In each case the fund use and the student publications won, and the funding continued. The *Exposure,* of Boston University, a private university, could not convince a court to intervene and require the university to provide funds. The university said it would if a faculty censor could approve copy, but student staff members wouldn't put up with that prior restraint.

The most significant case involved the University of Minnesota. Its president had made a mandatory student fee refundable to students not pleased with the *Daily*'s content. This followed an intense fuss after the *Daily* had produced an especially offensive end-of-the-year joke edition. Late in 1983, the U.S. Eighth Circuit Court of Appeals awarded the *Daily* $183,000 for legal fees and for lost student fee income. The court established a strong principle: The motivation of the university, based on unhappiness with content and in response to political pressures, was an unconstitutional infringement upon First Amendment protection.

Rutgers University and the National Association of State Land Grant Colleges and Universities became alarmed when six students of the Camden campus sued to eliminate a mandatory student fee to support the political activities of the campus Public Interest Research Group (PIRG). This partisan agency has not persevered in court actions about its funding. The university officials feared that cutting off PIRG would jeopardize funding of other student activities, including student publications. The U.S. court of appeals ruled against the mandatory fee, saying the PIRG activities were not of sufficient educational value to justify setting aside other constitutional protections of the six students. This decision pertained only to PIRG and in no way affected student publications or other student activity funding. The Supreme Court in 1986 affirmed the appeals court decision without comment, so the narrowness of the decision was sustained.

Courts have ruled on three occasions that the University of North Carolina could fund its *Daily Tarheel* despite some objections to its content by some students.

The 3,000 student newspapers of college campuses are diverse and amazing. Some are the equivalent of very well written and edited large daily newspapers. Some are trivial gossip sheets. But they all function, and they all cost money. More than 90 percent receive fund allocations from college general funds or from mandatory student fees. Most publish advertising. Some utilize their extensive typesetting, layout, and printing facilities to earn additional income.

This data comes from a reading of Politella's 1977–1978 *Directory of the College Student Press in America.* Growth of the campus press is dramatically clear when the third edition of the *Directory* is compared with the fourth. The third edition indicates that 35 of the campus newspapers in Indiana, for example, received fund allocations or compulsory student fees, while only 4 did not. (Information was not available for four newspapers.)

A look backward to the practices of financing student publications can be found in a 1953 study of teachers colleges: 110 teachers colleges of the 122 from which data were available, or 90.1 percent, budgeted funds from a student activity fee to finance the student newspaper; 102, or 83.6 percent, used advertising income; 47, or 38.5 percent, sold subscriptions to alumni; 18, or 14.7 percent, received funds from faculty subscriptions; 17, or 13.9 percent, were granted funds from the regular college budget; 12, or 9.8 percent, sold subscriptions to students; and 3, or 2.5 percent, had other sources of income. Thirteen, or 10.7 percent, college newspapers received all their financial support from student fees or subscriptions; 51 papers, or 41.8 percent, combined student contributions with advertising revenue; 51, or 41.8 percent, found it necessary to add other sources to the student contribution and the advertising revenue available; 7, or 5.7 percent, of the papers received their total funds from sources other than students and advertisers. Altogether, 102, or 83.6 percent, of the 122 student newspapers made use of a student activity fee arrangement and advertising to finance their program; 20, or 16.3 percent, of the colleges did not use advertising or a student activity fee in their financing.

In 1973 the Associated Collegiate Press evaluated 119 college newspapers and found they all received university fund allocations or mandatory student fee income; however, 6 did receive a substantial amount also for subscription sales, and 91 carried advertising.

Lee VanBremen conducted a survey of the financing of college and university newspapers for a doctoral dissertation at the University of Connecticut in 1973. He found that advertising and student fees were the two main sources of income for student newspapers. Neither source, he said, had a greater proportional increase than the other in a six-year period.

The *Diamondback,* of the University of Maryland, compiled data from 37 of the top 50 college daily newspapers ranked by circulation for 1974–1975. Twenty-seven received student fee money, 37 carried advertising, and 23 received other income, including college appropriations, printing services, and subscription sales. Michigan State's $708,800 advertising income led the group that year; several student daily newspapers are now near the million-dollar advertising revenue level. Even so, mandatory student fee money or a subsidy from general funds continues to be an important part of financing even these large newspaper operations.

Virtually every college or university, public or private, large or small, should maintain a student yearbook. Values received by the institution and its students make the cost an excellent investment for the students for many years.

A yearbook records in words and good pictures the events of a year in the lives of students and the institution. The tone and significance of that year with its unique qualities can be perpetuated magnificently if student staff understand the nature of a yearbook and that yearbook is adequately and stably financed.

The tradition of an excellent yearbook inspires students to present the institution in the best light possible with the greatest accuracy and poignancy. What better tangible evidence of the greatness of a college or university would any student journalist, adviser, administrator, public relations official, or board member want taken from the campus into the eyes of parents, patrons, alumni, or the publics important to the institution? This will happen if the yearbook program is recognized as important and worthwhile by the institution. It will happen if a knowledgeable and dedicated adviser is available to the staff. It will happen if the staff has on-campus training sessions, attends yearbook conferences and workshops, and has the challenge of excellence before it at all times.

Of course, all the guarantees of press freedom accorded citizens apply to the contents of the student yearbook. Once an editor is appointed in a public institution, that editor is the person whose First Amendment rights prevail.

A yearbook should contain from 160 to 640 pages. It should have a strong cover physically speaking and should be well bound to last indefinitely. Kooky content and kooky mechanics are simply not worth the effort or the money. The content should be imaginative and creative with appropriate theme, layout, and editorial tone. Four-color pictures should appear on from 8 to 72 pages, and spot color and other special effects should be utilized.

Each term, a mandatory sum can be assessed from the fees paid by students or from general funds of the institution to provide adequate financing for the student yearbook. With today's prices, this should amount to about $5 per quarter per student, or about $8 per semester; this assessment would generate sufficient funds to provide a copy of a yearbook to each and every student who wants one at no additional cost to the student. Usually, three-fourths of the students ask for copies.

Dario Politella, an early president of College Media Advisers, compiles data for the *Directory of the College Student Press in America,* which is published by the Oxbridge Company. The sixth edition, issued in 1986, provided an overview of the campus student press. It listed student media from 3,610 institutions, including four-year colleges, two-year community colleges, satellite campuses, and special schools within universities.

Politella estimated that at least 10,000 student publications served more than 12 million college students. The field was a volatile one, with publications dying, being created, consolidating, and changing their nature and names. Of America's campuses 84 percent had student newspapers, 47 percent had yearbooks, and 42 percent had magazines.

He found 1,221 magazines, the most changeable of all. These included literary, general interest, news, special interest, and technical publications. The least popular student magazine type for the 1980s was humor magazines, probably the victims of triteness. The magazines printed nearly 2.5 million copies and had a combined budget of more than $3 million. Two-thirds were printed offset and a fifth used color. Funds to maintain the publications came from advertising in 13 percent of the magazines; individual copies were sold by 5.4 percent of the magazines, and 57 percent had allocations from college or student activity funds. An additional 59 percent had to find additional income.

Politella found 1,365 yearbooks in 1986. They produced 1.7 million copies and had a combined budget of $16.3 million. They were almost all printed offset. Book size averaged 210 pages, at an average cost of $9.66 per book. About 43 percent had color printing. For financing, less than a third of the yearbooks carried advertising or sold individual copies, while 63 percent of the yearbooks were supported by university or student fee allocations.

The *Cactus,* of the University of Texas at Austin, was the largest yearbook with 736 pages and 12,000 copies. The three service academies produced yearbooks with more than 600 pages.

The nearly 2,500 newspapers produced more than 8 million copies for their combined issue runs and budgeted about $60 million annually. All but about 7 percent were printed offset, and a fourth included color printing. Three-fourths of the newspapers carried advertising, and only 14 percent sold individual copies, while 70 percent received funds from university or student fee allocations. Even so, 39 percent of the newspapers had to find additional income sources, such as job printing services. More than half of the College Media Advisers student publications had faculty advisers, but fewer than 2 percent bothered to copyright their contents.

The college yearbook has strengthened appreciably during the last five years. In the 1960s, yearbooks lost favor because of the turmoil and the withdrawal attitudes of college students in that era and because some administrators believed yearbooks were an unnecessary expense. But yearbooks are coming back strongly. They have been reestablished on some campuses where they had been discontinued. Many college students are now insisting that there be a yearbook. This means that yearbooks are being published on about half of the campuses; there were probably 1,800 of them in 1989. Yearbooks have benefited from the new technology and the desktop publishing facilities of the 1980s. Many staffs are now setting type and doing page makeup. This has improved production schedules and quality as well as reducing prices. A College Media Advisers yearbook workshop each summer, as well as national and regional conferences during the year, have made a contribution to good yearbooks.

College Media Advisers monitor the operation of college student publications with frequent surveys and studies. As part of these efforts, Lillian Lodge Kopenhaver, a former president of the organization and associate chair of the department of journalism at Florida International University, and Ronald E. Spielberger, headquarters manager for College Media Advisers at Memphis State University, completed a thorough study of the financing patterns of college student publications in 1987.[4] Here is their report.

The small college and university student media operation continues to be the norm across the United States, even though almost one-fifth of college newspapers publish daily, and more than one-tenth have a budget of $500,000 or more annually. In fact, 13 newspapers, or slightly less than 5%, have financial operations of more than $1 million a year.

However, the typical media operation is much different. More than two-thirds of college and university newspapers (195) publish weekly or less frequently; more than one-half (79) of the nation's yearbooks have 300 or fewer pages, and about one-half (38) of the magazines publish only one issue a year.

These figures and the trends indicated are very close to the results of a 1984 survey of the membership College Media Advisers printed in the Fall 1984 issue of College Media Review which sought to provide a profile of the finances and demographics of college and university student media. The 1987 study replicates that 1984 survey to provide an update as we move toward the decade of the 1990s.

Profile of 1987 Respondents

About half the respondents were from media operations at public four-year colleges (47.2% or 159), while private four-year institutions account for almost another one-third (30% or 101). Two-year colleges make up almost one-fourth: public (20.8% or 70) and private (2.1% or 7). Nearly half the colleges and universities responding (47.3% or 160) have enrollments of fewer than 7,500 students; 10.7% (36) have more than 25,000.

The number of employees supervised has generally decreased from 1984, with one-fifth (20.8% or 66) of those advising or managing student media reporting 1–2 employees as compared to 36% in 1984. Only 6.3% (20) have 12 or more employees, a decrease from 19.8% in 1984; 2.2% (7) have 21 or more.

In contrast, more than half (51.7% or 164) supervise no full-time employees.

Newspapers

More campus newspapers publish weekly than anything else (38.4% or 112); about one-third (28.4% or 83) publish less frequently. Dailies account for fewer than one-fifth of all campus newspapers (18.2% or 53), with 82.7% (43) of the dailies at four-year institutions.

All two-year college newspapers responding publish weekly or less frequently. Of the public two-year schools, 40.3% (27) print weekly and all seven of the private two-year college papers publish less frequently than weekly.

More than one-half of all campus newspapers (50.9% or 140) have revenues of $25,000 or less; more than half of these papers (52.1% or 73) publish on less than a weekly basis, while the rest are weeklies.

Slightly more than one-fourth (26.9% or 74) report revenues of $10,000 or less, a decrease from 31.6% in 1984. Nearly one-third (32.4% or 89) have revenues of more than $100,000, an increase from 27.5% in 1984.

Also showing an increase over 1984 are the number of papers with annual budgets in excess of $500,000, 12.7% or 35 in 1987 as opposed to 9.8% in 1984. In 1987, 13 dailies (4.7%) report budgets of more than $1 million.

Nearly all newspapers with revenues of more than $100,000 are at public four-year colleges (80.7% or 71); the rest are at private four-year schools (19.3% or 17). Very few newspapers with budgets of $10,000 or less are at public four-year colleges (5.6% or 7); however, 36.3% (29) of private four-year college newspapers fall into this category.

Most two-year college newspapers also have similar budgets: 71.4% (5) of the public schools. Of those operations having budgets of $1 million or more annually, 83.3% (10) are at public four-year colleges; the others are at private four-year schools.

Sources of newspaper revenue vary. Almost all college and university papers (93.5% or 273) report advertising revenue, a significant increase from the 84.7% in 1984. More than one-half (58.8% or 151) have 50% or more of their funding from advertising, an increase of 8.5% over 1984.

Eleven newspapers (4.3%) are totally funded by advertising. At the other end of the scale, 12.5% (32) receive 10% or less of their budget from advertising.

Most (81.1% or 99) public four-year papers have half or more of their revenue from ads, an increase from 75.3% in 1984. This is also the case for nearly one-half (45% or 36) of private four-year colleges, 25.5% (13) of public two-year colleges and 40% of private two-year schools; all represent increases from 1984. Of the 11 newspapers totally funded by advertising, 10 are at public four-year colleges and one is at a private four-year institution.

Nearly half of the college newspapers (49.3% or 143) receive money from student activities fees, a decrease from 55.9% in 1984. Almost half of these (48.6% or 70) receive 50% or more of their money from this source, an increase from 32.7% in 1984, and 5.6% (8) are totally funded by activities fees.

Of those fully funded, one is at a public four-year institution and seven are at public two-year colleges.

Public two-year colleges depend heavily on student activities fees for revenue; 43.3% (29) receive half or more of their funding from this source. Private two-year colleges follow with 28.6% (2) receiving 50% or more. At four-year institutions, private colleges report 21.8% (19) similarly funded.

Public colleges depend the least on student activities fees, with 15.5% (20) receiving half or more of their revenue from this source. These statistics show a significant decrease from percentages reported in the 1984 study for private four-year colleges (46.2%) and private two-year schools (50%).

Another revenue source for campus newspapers is funding from the college or university. More than one-fourth of all papers (29.4% or 100) receive money from the institution; 4.7% (16) secure their total revenue from this source and nearly one-fifth (17.9% or 61) receive 50% or more of their funds from the college.

Of those papers that receive half or more of their revenue from the institution, all categories except private two-year colleges show significant increases from 1984. Two-year colleges have the highest percentages of such funding: private, 57.1% (4) and public, 31.3% (21).

Private four-year institutions also report a significant number being so funded, 31% (27). Public four-year colleges have the lowest percentage (7.8% or 10).

Of those totally funded by the institution, seven are at public two-year colleges, three at public four-year colleges and four at private four-year institutions.

Only 19% (55) of campus papers sell subscriptions, all but five of those report it is less than one-third of their income.

Very few operations (10% or 29) receive student government funding. Of those who do, only 4.1% (12) receive half or more of their funds from this source.

Yearbooks

Most of the nation's college and university yearbooks (54.9% or 79) have 300 or fewer pages, while only 8.3% (12) have more than 500 pages. On either end of the scale, 7.6% (11) print 100 or fewer pages and 3.5% (5) print more than 600. Of the 12 largest books, those with more than 500 pages, all are at public four-year institutions. All nine of the two-year college books responding have 200 or fewer pages.

Nearly half of all yearbooks (42% or 53) have revenues of $25,000 or less, and 23% (29) operate on $10,000 or less. More than three-fourths (77.8% or 7) of the two-year college books have $10,000 or less revenue.

At four-year colleges, nearly two-thirds (63% or 29) of the private school books and nearly one-fourth (23.3% or 17) of the public school books have revenues of $25,000 or less. Fewer than one-fifth of the yearbooks (16.7% or 21) have revenues of more than $100,000; of those, 81% (14) are at public four-year colleges and four are at private four-year schools. Two books at public universities report revenues in excess of $300,000.

The two greatest sources of revenue of college and university yearbooks are sales of books (48.6% or 72) and student activities fees (50% or 74).

More than one-third of the college yearbooks (34.5% or 51) receive at least half their revenue from sales, and four books, three of which are at public four-year colleges and one at a private four-year college, are totally funded in this manner.

More than one-third (39.2% or 58) receive 50% or more of their revenue from student activities fees; 14.2% (21) of the books are totally funded in this way. Of the latter, 12 are at public four-year colleges, six at private four-year schools, two at public two-year colleges and one at a private two-year institution.

Nearly half (47.5% or 38) of the public four-year books are supported 50% or more by sales; 20.4% (11) of the private four-year college yearbooks also have sales as a major source of revenue, while two private two-year college books also receive more than 50% of their revenue from sales. Three-fourths (3) of the private two-year college yearbooks are funded by student activities fees, as are 60% (30) of the public two-year books. At nearly half (46.3% or 25) of the private four-year colleges and more than one-third (36.3% or 29) of the public four-year institutions, half or more of the yearbook revenue comes from activities fees. Those figures represent a significant increase from 27.3% in 1984 for public colleges.

Advertising sales are the next largest source for yearbook financing, with 37.8% (56) reporting such revenue. This is an increase from the 1984 figure of 31.7%. Only one book at a private four-year college receives 50% or more of its revenue from this source, however.

Photo and page sales rank next on the list of sources of income for yearbooks (35.8% or 53), though few (2.7% or 4) receive 50% or more of their funding from it.

College funding provides revenue for one-fourth (26.4% or 39) of the nation's books, an increase from the 1984 figure of 20.8%. Eight books are totally funded in this manner, four at public four-year colleges, three at private four-year schools, and one at a private two-year institution.

Magazines

Almost one-half (48.4% or 45) of the magazines in college and universities are literary in nature; 29% (27) are general interest and 2.2% (2) are devoted to news.

More than half the magazines at four-year institutions are literary in nature; public four-year colleges have 51.1% (23) in this category and private four-year schools report 54.5% (18). Next highest are general interest: public four-year schools, 28.9% (13) and private four-year schools, 21.1% (7). Both news magazines were reported by private four-year colleges.

At public two-year colleges, more magazines are general interest (58.3% or 7) than literary (25% or 3), and the private two-year colleges reported one literary magazine and one listed as "other."

Most magazines are published once a year (41.3% or 38), with 2 to 3 issues a year a close second (39.1% or 36); 10 magazines are published 4 to 5 times a year, three 6 to 8 times a year and five 9 times or more.

Most two-year college magazines are published once a year; 58.3% (7) at public two-year colleges fall into this category as do two-thirds (2) at private two-year schools. At public two-year colleges another one-third (4) publish 2 to 3 issues and one publishes 4 to 5 issues a year.

At public four-year colleges 18 magazines publish one issue a year, while 18 others publish 2 to 3 issues, six publish 4 to 5 issues and two publish 9 or more.

At private four-year colleges, 13 magazines print 2 to 3 issues a year, 11 publish once a year, three publish 6 to 8 issues, and five print 9 or more issues annually. All those publishing 9 or more times a year have budgets of under $20,000.

Only 10.6% (10) of the magazines have 16 or fewer pages; two-fifths (41.5% or 39) have between 17–32 pages and one-fifth (21.3% or 20) print 49 pages or more. All magazines with 49 or more pages were reported by four-year colleges.

A clear majority of student magazines (71.6% or 58) report budgets of $5,000 or less. This includes all the private two-year magazines (3), 80% (20) of private four-year magazines, 66.1% (8) of public two-year and 65.9% (27) of public four-year magazines.

Only three (3.7%) have budgets of $20,000 or more, two of which are at public four-year schools and one at a public two-year college; all are general interest magazines. One of the public four-year magazines has a budget of $50,001 or more and is published 4 to 5 times a year.

Advertising revenues fund more magazines than any other source (40.9% or 38), an increase from 37.7% in 1984; however, only 8.6% (8) are totally funded in this manner. That includes seven public four-year college magazines.

Student activities fees subsidize 38.7% (36) of the campus magazines, a decrease from 45.9% in 1984. More than one-fifth (21.5% or 20) are totally subsidized in this manner; nine are at public four-year colleges, seven at private four-year schools, three at public two-year colleges and one at a private two-year institution.

College funding is another significant source of revenue for 36.6% of college magazines, up from 27.9% in 1984. Slightly more than one-third of these magazines receive 50% or more of their funding from college subsidies, and 26.9% (25) of all magazines are totally subsidized by their institutions, a significant increase from 15% in 1984.

Two other sources of funds are minimal: 16.1% (15) sell the magazine, and 7.5% (7) receive some revenue from student government. One private four-year college magazine is totally funded by sales and three magazines are totally funded by student government, two at public four-year colleges and one at a private two-year school.

Media Operations Patterns

The patterns that emerged when examining college and university student media across the country during the 1984 survey remain fairly constant in 1987, with a few exceptions.

In 1984, student activities fees were the major source of revenue for campus media, funding more than half the campus newspapers and slightly less than half the college and university yearbooks and magazines.

Advertising revenues increased for all print publications as a major source of funds. In addition, funding from the colleges or universities also increased.

The second pattern evident in campus media operations in 1984 was that most were of a relatively small size. That status has not changed in 1987. Nearly two-thirds of college and university newspapers still publish weekly or less frequently, and more than half still have a budget of $25,000 or less.

A majority of campus yearbooks still have 300 or fewer pages. Nearly one-half of student magazines (an increase from 1984) publish one issue per year and nearly two-thirds (also an increase from 1984) have $5,000 or less in budget.

A third pattern in 1984 was that more than two-thirds of student media were advised by individuals who had been in the business eight or fewer years, in their present jobs three or fewer years, and in a position without tenure. The same is true in 1987.

Small, aggressive campus media operations continue to be the standard across the nation in 1987, just as they were earlier in the 1980s. One trend is clear, however; in all instances, college and university print and broadcast operations are continuing to seek greater self-sufficiency by securing more revenue through advertising.

Over the years, in many surveys and studies, the data about financing college student publications remain consistent. During the past 20 years several publications have been weakened when administrative officials and student government officers, because of disagreement with publications content, reduced the funds because they might be convenient for other uses. This squeeze has made publication improvement difficult. Indeed, several college student yearbooks were bankrupted. A yearbook is difficult to establish; however, students in several colleges have tried and are trying to resurrect their yearbooks.

Budgeting officials of colleges should understand the need for adequate and stable financing of student publications. They should note an additional pattern emerging during the 1980s. Student publications are relying more on allocations from general university funds and less on funds generated by student activity fees. The publications have found college administrators much more reasonable and helpful than politicized or ambitious student government officials. The total funding, using either or both of these sources, is higher now than it was in the 1970s.

CHAPTER 4

Selling
Subscriptions

A frequent theme of advocates of no student fee or university allocations to student publications is that the publications should earn their circulation by selling subscriptions, like the commercial press. Of course, there are no commercial yearbooks published for a community to buy, so no analogy can be drawn for that type of publication.

A yearbook staff must contract for a variety of services about one year before the book is to be produced. The amount involved in these contracts can be many thousands of dollars. If the funds needed to meet these commitments come primarily from yearbook sales, the staff is gambling on a sales level high enough to establish a budget. One lazy student, a decline in enrollment, a late delivery from the printer, or other catastrophes can ruin that budget. Who pays then? Individually sold yearbooks should sell for about $20 to $35 each. This is a high price, forced by the small number printed. If the yearbook prints 5,000 or more copies, it can prorate charges across this number, so that the cost per book with high quality and process color is not great. It's very difficult to sell 5,000 yearbooks at $20 each in any college. The costs of producing yearbooks of quality appear in Table 4.1.

Normally, a yearbook may earn from $4 to $8 per copy from earnings such as advertising, space charges, or contractual premiums.

A college or university with 5,000 students could produce a 352-page yearbook if $10 was allocated from each student's fees per year or by an equal sum from other allocations. Smaller colleges would have to allocate more money from fees or reduce the size of and special effects in their books. Larger colleges could expand size and effects with no budget strain. If fees were not allocated, each student would have to

Table 4.1. Yearbook Budgets

Number of Copies	Number of Pages	Minimum Production Costs	Amount to Be Provided Per Copy from Sales, Fees, or Allocations
1,000	352	$ 35,000	$30
2,000	368	50,000	20
3,000	384	65,000	17
4,000	400	80,000	16
5,000	416	95,000	15
6,000	432	115,000	15
7,000	448	130,000	13
8,000	464	140,000	13
9,000	492	150,000	12
10,000	508	160,000	12
11,000	524	170,000	11
12,000	540	180,000	11

pay up to $25 for a yearbook, because of reduced circulation, or twice as much as in the fee allocation system. If the yearbook is considered a luxury or plaything by the university, no doubt funds will not be allocated, and whatever yearbook exists will be skimpy and live precariously in semibankruptcy.

If a college understands that a yearbook can be a thrilling pictorial record of a year in the life of its students and its history, it can comprehend the cohesive communicative value of such a publication. If communications, or better communications, are important to the college, it deserves and needs a well-edited student yearbook.

Selling subscriptions for college newspapers is an even worse plan. Most commercial newspapers do sell subscriptions (some do not). Daily newspapers charge readers $1.50 to $3.50 per week. *USA Today* cost $2.50 for five issues each week in 1992.

After newspapers pay the costs of the carriers or sales contractor, the distribution truckers, the office staff, the record keepers, and so on, the net income from the circulation dwindles to very little. Newspapers seldom receive as much as 25 percent of their income from circulation.

Here are two college press case studies:

Paper A was located in a large university with 40,000 students. It managed to sell about 8,000 subscriptions annually. Student subscriptions were 40 cents per week, $6 per semester, or $12 per student per year (summer terms were extra).

Paper B was located in a middle-size university with 15,000 students. It distributed 14,000 copies daily on campus distribution racks. It received a student fee allocation of about $2 per semester, or $4 per year per student. Thus the paper B cost each student $8 less than paper A.

Both papers were well written and edited. The level of communication value of each paper was excellent. Unfortuately, paper A, no matter how hard it tried, could not raise the level of circulation. That level has remained at the same percentage for nearly 40 years. Paper B served its campus much better.

This isn't the real tragedy for paper A. Each year, it sells about $100,000 to $110,000 worth of subscriptions. But to sell, account, service, deliver, and police these subscriptions, paper A has to spend about $100,000. This leaves a balance of less than $10,000 to produce the paper.

Paper B receives about $90,000 annually from student fees. It spends less than $10,000 to distribute its paper. Thus it nets more than $80,000 annually to produce and improve the paper.

Similar data would develop from other comparisons. As a result of the small return from subscription income, some papers rely on advertising income only and distribute papers on distribution racks. This increased circulation justifies higher ad rates and improves the communicative function of the paper. Such a plan can work in situations where a large community of retailers need the campus paper to reach a large student enrollment and a well-paid advertising staff is employed. In middle-size and small colleges, the advertising-only plan would not be sufficient.

If student fee or other allocations were not available, many colleges would have skimpy papers with small circulations. Ambitious staffs might turn to sensational content to stir up readership and sell a few more subscriptions. This effort has never worked effectively for either student or commercial newspapers.

Commercial newspapers do not experience great fluctuations in circulation. The strength of their circulation depends upon home-delivered copies in the city and its immediate retail trading area. This is the circulation advertisers want. A careful check is made of this quality circulation by the Audit Bureau of Circulations, a national agency. Circulation is the result of several factors, one of which is the highly skilled and well-paid circulation director. In all but a few cities, the commercial paper is the only newspaper available to the community. Readers shop the ads constantly and buy the paper for them. People develop the newspaper habit, which means they subscribe automatically. Most commercial newspapers reach 80–95 percent of all possible subscribers in their communities.

College newspapers cannot develop that percentage because their clientele is far more mobile than that of a typical town. Average longevity of a college student is about two years. It's hard to settle into many habits during that time.

Many college students are housed in private homes, dormitories, fraternity houses, or sorority houses. An amazing variety of restrictive rules about selling subscriptions or delivering papers in such housing units exist in the 3,600 colleges and their communities. These restrictions are generally not a problem for a commercial newspaper.

It is unwise to expect a campus newspaper to do with a handful of students what it takes a complement of full-time circulation executives, bookkeepers, managers, supervisors, drivers, carriers, and newstand dealers to manage for commercial papers. There simply isn't enough time or money available on the campus to do it that way.

CHAPTER 5

Incorporation

Several writers have apparently been convinced that there was a trend toward incorporation among college student newspapers throughout the 1970s. They ascribe to incorporation a magic that they believe assured total editorial independence and freedom, gritty financing through learning to live in the marketplace, and sure escape from ornery and repressive college administrators. By 1988, the number of incorporated publications had increased to about 80.

Truthfully, incorporation in and of itself doesn't mean any of these.

One College Media Advisers study found 13 colleges where both the newspaper and the yearbook were incorporated. In 26 colleges only the newspaper was incorporated, and in 2 colleges only the yearbook was incorporated. A total of 54 publications were incorporated in 41 colleges. This was less than 4 percent of the nation's campus press. Twenty-two newspapers and 13 yearbooks that had never bothered with incorporation claimed total independence. No information could be found to refute that claim. Several points should be made about the incorporated publications. More than 40 of them had been incorporated for several years. The fact that a dozen or so might have incorporated during the last four or five years does not constitute a "trend."

Not all publications that have considered incorporation have decided to become incorporated.

The generally accepted interpretations of the functions of student publications are (1) vehicles for disseminating campus information and creative material, and editorializing; (2) mechanisms through which students learn. These interpretations by the North Dakota Board of Higher Education were adopted as proposed by the Committee on

Student Publications of the North Dakota State School of Sciences in 1970. The committee was asked to study the feasibility of separating campus publications from institutional responsibility.

Alternatives to school subsidization would of course include possible incorporation of the publication. While incorporation was not mentioned specifically in the report, the committee rejected the entire concept of complete autonomy from university influence.

The reasons for rejecting separation from the school of the publications included

1. The institution would suffer by the loss of a valuable learning tool — production of the publications themselves.

2. Loss of the interchange between students and instructors would further minimize the educational advantage of publications.

3. Institutions would still be identified in the public mind with the "underground" or independent publications; thus, separation would not eliminate a chief reason for the action — to eliminate embarrassing identification with the school.

4. Public pressure on the school to discipline or dismiss members of publication staffs would not necessarily decrease from establishment of "independent" publications.

5. A possible abuse of college authority looms in compelling all students (through fee subscriptions) to finance publications they may not choose to support. Assuming the avoidance of legal restrictions in attaining "independence," would not actual student reader influence on the editors become less involved?

6. "Irresponsibility" of student publications, the committee claims to have discovered, increases when the publications are forced off campus and removed from the influence of other students and/or administration.

7. Many publications (as borne out partially in the cases of the North Carolina Central University *Campus Echo* and the Columbia University *Daily Spectator*) quickly encounter financial difficulty and in some instances perish after separation from the institution.[1]

Publications at the University of Texas at Austin were incorporated for 50 years, but when the corporation expired in 1971, the university reorganized the publications as auxiliary enterprises.

Efforts to force independence and incorporation on the *Daily Nexus* at the University of California at Santa Barbara were rejected by the student staff.

Corporations are legally established according to specific steps outlined by state laws. Corporations must file articles of incorporation. Within these articles a series of provisions can be included. If any part of the articles stipulates a university relationship or connection, the student newspaper cannot be considered independent even though it is incorporated. The articles can specify the precise university relationship, fund allocations, and everything else. Incorporation thus could mean dependence or independence.

The strength of the independence provided by incorporation can be found in the type of incorporation accorded almost all student publications. There are regular profit-making business corporations, and there are nonprofit corporations. The latter is a simple structure and easy to set up and maintain. Educational agencies can qualify as nonprofit corporations. Commercial newspapers cannot. If student publications are clearly related to the educational nature and structure of their university, they can qualify. All but a few of the campus publications are nonprofit corporations, which means their relationship to the university entitles them to special treatment. If a student publication qualifies as a nonprofit corporation, it does so because of its relationship to the university, not because of independence from it.

Colleges follow a variety of plans for the operation of student publications, including:

1. Organized as an activity funded and controlled by the student government agency.

2. Organized as an activity funded by a club or a group of students.

3. Organized as a formal instructional laboratory funded and controlled by an academic department such as journalism. Faculty members may serve as editors, supervising students enrolled in formal journalism classes that are assigned aspects of the publication's productions.

4. Organized as an informal learning laboratory associated with an academic department but controlled by the student staff.

5. Organized as a special enterprise, primarily for financial operation, sometimes called an auxiliary enterprise or a self-liquidating enterprise.

6. Incorporated as a nonprofit corporation as a closely related or actual part of the host college.

7. Incorporated as a nonprofit corporation only loosely related to the host college.

8. Incorporated as a regular profit-making corporation only loosely related to the host college.

9. Organized as an administrative function funded and controlled by the college administration, which designates itself as publisher and editor.

10. Organized as a public relations publication catering to both internal and external publics.

11. Organized as a counseling activity carrying out student personnel projects.

12. Organized as a separate legal entity, either incorporated or unincorporated.

On a limited number of campuses, a plan developed to declare the campus press independent of the college, set it up as an independent corporation, move it off the campus or perhaps charge it rent for campus facilities, ignore it, disavow any responsibility for its contents, and even proclaim that such a plan was a distinct advantage or favor for the campus journalists. Colleges generally rejected this plan since they found little advantage in it. Legally they found it difficult to dissociate from the student publications, and financially the student publications had difficulties. More important was the philosophical abandonment of the concept of a free press which is an important part of American education.

Actually, each of the 12 plans listed above can provide for a free student press, and each can provide for a rigidly controlled student press. It depends on attitudes and agreed-upon principles and guidelines. On several campuses, a publications committee or board develops such principles and guidelines.

One state court found that where a publishing operation such as a university press is incorporated as a distinct entity separate from the state and money from publishing activities is kept separate from general university funds, the university will maintain its sovereign immunity, but the publishing operation will be subject to suit; *Applewhite* v. *Memphis State University,* 405 S.W.2d 190 (Tenn. 1973).

If a "university press" can be organized as a separate entity from the university itself for the purposes of publishing scholarly periodicals and books, there can be no doubt that student publications can also be organized as separate legal entities. This separateness requires that the funds of the publications not be intermingled with those of the university, which may contract to pay or allocate sums of money to the publication for providing specified numbers of copies for campuswide distribution or advertising space.

Incorporation can certainly establish the separate legal entity of a student publication. Nonincorporation also could establish such status if the publication actually operated as a separate legal entity.

During the 1970s a series of articles appeared heralding incorporation of the campus student newspaper as a method of achieving editorial independence from the host university, its administration, its faculty, or its student government. A few campus newspapers that had been severely abused by university administrators did incorporate with this hope. In some cases this plan provided considerable improvement; in others there was no improvement or even a worsening of the lot of the publication.

Dario Politella, of the University of Massachusetts, has been compiling data for directories of the college student press for several years. In the 2,581 colleges reporting data for the 1986 *Directory of the College Student Press in America* he estimated there could be as many as 10,000 student media. Fewer than 1 percent were incorporated. The National Council of College Publication Advisers (now College Media Advisers, Inc.) evaluated 61 college publication systems that claimed to be "independent" of the host university.

A careful study of the articles of incorporation of the student publications and other campus procedures indicates that incorporation in and of itself is no guarantee of freeing the content of the student newspaper from the control of the university or its agents. Very restrictive provisions can be (and have been) written into articles of incorporation. Indeed, incorporation appears in some instances as a deliberate way to require student editors to comply with the directives of an oppressive board of directors. When litigation occurs, courts routinely pierce the corporate veil to determine the locus of content control to determine legal liability.

In contrast to this restrictive approach has been a careful plan to establish an effective corporate structure to provide for the production and financing of strong student publications.

The most important goal of the publication is to become a separate legal entity via incorporation of other organizational structures.

The *Daily Californian* staff found itself in a serious conflict with the University. As a result the paper became an incorporated operation. Although the paper considers itself independent, changes in its bylaws must have the approval of the university.

An effective model of a student publishing operation can be found at the University of Illinois and the University of Maryland. Each of these corporations includes the student daily newspaper, yearbook, magazines, and radio stations. The Illini Publishing Company has been in business for several decades. Maryland Media, Inc., is much younger.

The Illini Publishing Company described the function of its corporation as follows: "A well managed student publishing company located on a campus of a great university must have stability, it should have a large degree of autonomy from the administration of the university and from student political organizations and it must have the ability to provide for its own future."

A student publishing company should involve its students in both the day-to-day operation and long-range plans and goals. A well-managed publishing company will encourage a flow of ample communication within each department and between the various departments. Decisions should be made with as many of the pertinent facts as can be assembled. Ideally a student publishing company should work towards financial independence. It should continually set aside some earnings for future development. Most importantly, a well-managed student publishing company should attract and hold dedicated professional staff members who will offer stability and support the efforts of the student editors, writers, photographers, designers, sales staff, and business staff.

If incorporation can really deliver editorial independence and financial stability to the campus student press, it seems odd that fewer than 100 universities have followed that path.

Each state has statutory provisions for the creation of corporations, profit or not-for-profit. The following information was taken from a collection of 40 of these state provisions so that persons unfamiliar with the not-for-profit world could become acquainted with detailed possibilities. By 1989 many states had enacted a new standard incorporation model suggested by a national commission. Steps necessary to incorporate require the services of an attorney. A reading of the following provisions should equip a student staff and an adviser to carry on a productive conversation with the attorney that would tailor the proposed corporation to the needs and circumstances of its student publications and its host college.

THE CHARTER AND OTHER DOCUMENTS

In every state, a nonprofit corporation must file articles of incorporation (or a similar document). The articles establish the legal authority of the corporation to exist and function. Various states will require, and in some cases suggest or permit, the following items, statements, or provisions to be included. Both requirements and permissive content vary greatly from state to state. (The appendix contains examples of actual incorporation charters in effect for 1989 for student publications.) All of the following should be checked.

Intention

Indication that the undersigned incorporation or incorporators execute the articles of incorporation pursuant to state law.

Name

The name of the corporation must include the word *corporation* or *incorporated* or one of the abbreviations thereof.

Status

Indication of nonprofit nature with a statement such as "this corporation is a nonprofit public benefit corporation and is not organized for the private gain of any person. It is organized under the provisions pertaining to an educational nonprofit corporation."

"Not-for-profit," as applied to corporations, means "any corporation which does not engage in any activities for the profit of its members and which is organized and conducts its affairs for purposes other than the pecuniary gain of its members."

Purpose

The nonprofit corporation for student publications is one with educational purposes similar to those of its host college or university.

• It is not sufficient merely to indicate that the purpose of the corporation is to produce student publications. The purpose must state that the educational nature of the corporation is to train or educate students in journalism publications and to prepare for professional competence in journalism publications, broadcast media, or related professional goals or media.

• If the intent of the corporation is to assure student editors freedom of the press, the charter and bylaws must state that the directors, incorporators, members, officers, or agents do not desire or establish the mechanism to control the editorial content. The purpose of the corporation is to arrange for the publishing of student publications so that the editor may control content and exercise free press rights. If this statement is not included, the student staff must submit their judgments to the directors and officers (and perhaps "members") if they are specified.

Statements similar to the following may also be required.

• This corporation is organized and operated exclusively for educational purposes within the meaning of Section 501(c)(3) of the Federal Internal Revenue.

• Notwithstanding any other provision of these articles, the corporation shall not carry on any other activities not permitted to be carried on (a) by a corporation exempt from federal income tax under Section 501(c)(3) of the Internal Revenue Code or (b) by a corporation contributions to which are deductible under Section 170(c)(2) of the Internal Revenue Code.

• The property of this corporation is irrevocably dedicated to educational purposes, and no part of the net income or assets of this corporation shall ever dissolve to the benefit of any director, officer, or member thereof or to the benefit of any private person. Upon the dissolution or winding up of the corporation, its assets remaining after payments, or provision for payment, of all debts and liabilities of this corporation shall be distributed to a nonprofit fund, foundation, or corporation which is organized and operated exclusively for educational purposes and which has established its tax exempt status under Section 501(c)(3) of the Internal Revenue Code.

• No part of the net earnings of the corporation shall inure to the benefit of, or be distributable to its members, directors, officers, or other private persons, except that the corporation shall be authorized and empowered to pay reasonable compensation for services rendered and to make payments and distributions in furtherance of the purposes set forth. No substantial part of the activities of the corporation shall be the carrying on of propaganda, or otherwise attempting to influence legislation, and the corporation shall not participate in, or intervene in (including the publishing or distribution of statements), any political campaign on behalf of any candidate for public office. Notwithstanding any other provision of these articles, the corporation shall not carry on any other activities not permitted to be carried on (a) by a corporation exempt from federal income tax under Section 501(c)(3) of the Internal Revenue Code of 1954 (or the corresponding provision of any future United States Internal Revenue Law) or (b) by a corporation contributions to which are deductible under Section 170(c)(2) of the Internal Revenue Code of 1954 (or the corresponding provision of any future United States Internal Revenue Law).

• Upon the dissolution of the corporation, the Board of Directors shall, after paying or making provision for the payment of all the liabilities of the purposes of the corporation, dispose of all its assets exclusively for the purposes of the corporation in such manner, or to such organization organized and operated exclusively for charitable, educational, religious, or scientific purposes as shall at the time qualify as an exempt organization or organizations under Section 501(c)(3) of the Internal Revenue Code of 1954 (or the corresponding provision of any future United States Internal Revenue Law) as the Board of Directors shall determine. Any such assets not disposed of shall be disposed of by the Supreme Court of the county in which the principal office of the corporation is then located, exclusively for such purposes to such organization or organizations, as said Court shall determine, which are organized and operated exclusively for such purposes.

• Any provision which the incorporators may choose to insert to direct the conduct of the affairs of the corporation and any provision creating, dividing, limiting, and regulating the powers of the corporation, the directors, managers or trustees, and the members, including, but not limited to, provisions establishing classes of membership and limiting voting rights to one or more of such classes.

Period of Existence

The period during which the corporation shall continue is to be indicated. It may be "perpetual" or a limited period of time. The place and probable dates of the annual meeting of the corporation may be required. Indication of the fiscal year dates may be required.

Resident Agent

The name and address of the corporation's resident agent for service of process must be provided. The address shall be a street or building.

Principal Office of the Corporation

The post office address of the principal office of the corporation must be provided. This shall be a street or building address.

Membership

If the corporation does not have members, that fact must be indicated. (This appears to be the best plan for student publications.) If the corporation does have members, the articles should indicate how they were selected and whatever qualifications membership requires.

A minimum of three persons may be required to have signed the membership list. Directors, or trustees, or incorporators may be included in the membership. If there are classes of members, that must be indicated. The rights, preference, limitations, and restrictions of classes should be included.

The voting rights of the classes of members should be indicated.

The corporation shall confer upon every member a certificate signed by the president (or vice president) and secretary (or assistant secretary) stating that he or she is a member of the corporation.

Directors

The exact names of the members of the board of directors must be provided. The number of directors must be indicated. If the exact number is not given, the minimum and maximum numbers must be indicated. The date of their election must be given.

The initial board of directors will serve until regular ones are selected by a regular election.

The minimum number of directors is three. Persons who serve as directors must be 18 years old or older.

Incorporators

The names and post office addresses of the corporation's incorporators must be given. One person may be the incorporator, or two or more may be incorporators.

Officers

The names, post office addresses, terms, methods of selection, and duties of officers should be included.

Statement of Property and Capital

A statement of the property and an estimate of the value thereof owned by and to be taken over by the corporation at or upon its incorporation must be provided. An indication of the dollar amount of the capital of the corporation should be given. A detailed budget may be required.

An indication of the corporation's intention to apply for state or federal tax exempt status may be required.

Bylaws or Constitution

A detailed set of rules for operation of the corporation should be devised. It may be required as part of or as an accompaniment to the articles. Provisions, consistent with the laws of the state, for the regulation and conduct of the affairs of the corporation, and creating, defining, limiting, or regulating the powers of the corporation, the directors, or the members of any class or classes of members should be included.

The charter should indicate how the bylaws are to be made, or amended, or rescinded. The charter should indicate who has the authority for making, altering, or rescinding bylaws.

Application

Three persons must sign the articles and indicate that the document is an application for incorporation. Written signatures should accompany the printed names of the incorporators. The written signatures must be certified by a notary. Some states provide printed forms; in some states business or stationery stores sell forms they have created; in some states the corporation may devise its own form.

The secretary of state or an agency under the secretary is normally the place to obtain forms, pay fees, obtain help, and file articles. Usually two copies of the articles or forms on 8½″ × 11″ paper must be submitted.

In addition to the articles of incorporation it may be necessary to submit the following documents preceding the filing, at the time of filing, or subsequently:

1. A telephone call to ask for a name search may be in order. The state corporation office will determine whether the name conflicts with existing names.

2. A written request for such a search may be required.

3. A written request for a 30-day name reservation should be submitted before the remaining steps are completed.

4. It may be necessary to request in writing an extension of this reservation.

5. It may be possible to transfer an already reserved name to the proposed corporation upon written request and agreement.

6. If an out-of-state corporation wishes to do business in the state, it must submit a written application to do so.

7. Checks for fees must be forwarded with each form.

8. A trust instrument may be required.

9. Legal advertising in newspapers may be required.

10. The bylaws or constitution may be required at the time the articles are filed.

11. A certificate of disclosure may be required.

12. A letter of transmittal may be required.

13. A form may be required as an application to serve as the corporation's agent.

14. An affidavit of the agent's agreement to serve as the corporation's agent may be required.

15. Application for exemption from state taxes may be required.

16. A certificate indicating adoption of the bylaws may be required.

17. Application for federal income tax exemption may be required.

18. A special form listing the corporation's property may be required.

19. A detailed description of proposed activities may be required.

Subsequent to chartering, the corporation may be involved with these steps:

1. A form may be required if the agent of the corporation changes.

2. A form may be required if the home office address changes.

3. If the agent resigns, a report may be required.

4. If the agent's office address changes, a report may be required.

5. Amendments of the articles of incorporation must be reported.

6. Amendments of the bylaws must be filed.

7. A merger with another corporation must be reported.

8. Consolidation with other corporations must be reported. The name assumed by the consolidated corporation must be cleared and filed.

9. An intent to dissolve the corporation must be filed.

10. If the corporation decides not to dissolve, a form revoking voluntary dissolution proceedings must be filed.

11. Formal articles of dissolution proceedings must be filed.

12. An application for surrendering the authority to operate in the state by an out-of-state corporation may be required.

13. A certificate of the name of the person having custody of the minutes of the corporation may be required.

14. An annual (or biennial) report is required.

15. An excuse from filing such reports may be possible.

16. The corporation must keep accurate financial records of its operations. These must be available for inspection.

17. Accurate minutes of all corporate meetings must be maintained and available for inspection.

18. The corporation must submit itself and its records to inspections by state officials according to state laws.

19. Officers and directors must attend hearings about the corporation by state officials.

20. The corporation may be required to submit an "annual exhibit."

21. Certificates of correction must be filed.

POWERS AND ACTIVITIES THAT NONPROFIT CORPORATIONS MAY BE PERMITTED

Nonprofit corporations may be permitted to carry out the following activities and operations under the powers authorizing such corporations in many states. However, laws in several states might not authorize many of these. The articles of incorporation can be used to deny any of them by specific written permission. State laws and regulations of the Internal Revenue Service might also negate some of them.

Charter for Articles of Incorporation
1. The corporation may exist perpetually.
2. The corporation may have perpetual use of its name.
3. The corporation may, however, specify the time of its existence in the articles of incorporation.
4. Specific powers authorized by state law may be enjoyed by the corporation unless the articles of incorporation specifically restrict such powers.
5. The corporation may amend its articles of incorporation by following the steps specified by state laws.

Bylaws
1. The corporation may make, alter, amend, or repeal bylaws not in conflict with the provisions of any state laws for the management of its property and the operation or regulation of its affairs.
2. The corporation may enact emergency bylaws as provided by state law.

Directors, Officers, Agents, Members, Employees
1. The corporation may increase or decrease by vote, as the bylaws may direct, the number of its directors so that the number may be at least three or any number in excess thereof.
2. The corporation may indemnify its directors, officers, employees, or agents.
3. The corporation may elect or appoint officers, agents, or subordinates, define their duties, and fix their compensations.
4. The corporation may reimburse its officers, directors agents, or employees for litigation costs.
5. The corporation may use its credit to assist its employees (but not its directors, officers, or agents).
6. The corporation may pay pensions, establish and carry out pensions, savings, trust plans, and provisions for its employees.

7. The corporation may lend money to its employees (but not to its directors, officers, or agents).

8. The corporation may assist its employees by means in addition to lending them money.

9. The corporation may admit members or associates and may sell or forfeit their interests in the corporation or may enforce the collection of dues from members and establish classes of members.

10. The corporation may decide not to have members.

11. The corporation may improve real or personal property or any interest therein, wherever located.

12. The corporation may acquire, enjoy, utilize, and dispose of patents, copyrights, trademarks, licenses, and any interests or rights therein.

13. The corporation may purchase and own obligations of the United States or of states, territories, districts, or municipalities.

14. The corporation may own shares, interests, or obligations of other corporations (profit or nonprofit), associations, partnerships, or individuals.

15. The corporation may sell, mortgage, lease, exchange, transfer, or dispose of its property and assets.

16. The corporation may transfer its real or personal property or an interest therein, wherever located.

17. The corporation may act as a trustee for property.

Operations and Activities

1. The corporation may have offices.

2. The corporation may transact any lawful business.

3. The corporation may conduct its affairs.

4. The corporation may have and exercise all powers necessary and convenient to effect any or all the purposes for which the corporation is organized.

5. The corporation may carry out its activities.

6. The corporation may do all other things proper to be done for the purpose of carrying into effect the objectives for which it is formed.

7. The corporation may exercise its powers or functions in any state or in any country.

8. The corporation may participate in any judicial, administrative, arbitrative, or other proceeding.

9. The corporation may contract or be contracted with.

10. The corporation may barter and exchange.

11. The corporation may expel any member or associate, or remove from office or appointment any director, officer, agent, or em-

ployee, as provided in the bylaws.

12. The corporation may procure for its benefit insurance on the life or physical or mental ability of any employee, officer, director, or agent whose death or disability might cause financial loss to the corporation, and to this end the corporation has an insurance interest in the lives of each of such persons.

The Corporate Seal

1. The corporation may have a seal.
2. The corporation may alter its seal at its pleasure.
3. The corporation may use its seal or a facsimile thereof at its pleasure and reproduce the seal by printing or other process.

Property

1. The corporation may own real or personal property or any interest therein, wherever located.
2. The corporation may receive real or personal property or any interest therein, wherever located.
3. The corporation may receive or take by gift real or personal property or any interest therein, wherever located.
4. The corporation may devise real or personal property or any interest therein, wherever located.
5. The corporation may otherwise acquire real or personal property or any interest therein, wherever located.
6. The corporation may lease real or personal property or any interest therein, wherever located.
7. The corporation may deal in and with real or personal property or any interest therein, wherever located.
8. The corporation may use real or personal property or any interest therein, wherever located.
9. The corporation may be a promoter, member, associate, or manager of a venture, trust, or other nonprofit enterprise.
10. The corporation may lend money for its corporate purposes and take and hold real and personal property as security for the payment of funds loaned or invested.
11. The corporation may give guarantees.
12. The corporation may incur liabilities.
13. The corporation may borrow money and set rates or interest as it may determine.
14. The corporation may reserve its obligations by mortgage or pledge all or any of its property, franchise, or income.
15. The corporation may issue notes, bonds, or other obligations.

16. The corporation is entitled to protection under estoppel and *ultra vires* procedures.

17. The corporation may provide proxy vote authorizations.

18. The corporation may guarantee or become security for the obligations of other nonprofit corporations.

19. The corporation may acquire the control of other nonprofit corporations and of business corporations.

20. The corporation may delegate control of its operations to other nonprofit corporations or agencies.

21. The corporation may form other nonprofit corporations.

22. The corporation may be a member of another nonprofit corporation.

23. The corporation may make donations for any charitable, scientific, educational, or welfare purpose or for aid for national emergency in time of war.

24. The corporation may make contributions to political candidates, parties, or issues to the extent permitted by law.

25. The corporation may merge and consolidate with other corporations, both for-profit and not-for-profit, domestic and foreign, provided that the surviving corporation is a nonprofit corporation.

26. The corporation may participate with others in any corporations, partnerships, limited partnership, joint venture, or other association of any kind, or in any transaction, undertaking, or agreement that the participating corporation would have power to conduct itself, whether or not the participation involves showing or delegation of control with or to others.

Although the foregoing lists of powers and rights are long, it should be noted that an individual, an organization or association, or a college student publication is legally empowered and has the right to do virtually every one of them without becoming actually or officially incorporated. Indeed, some states indicate that agencies connected with public colleges are not required to incorporate. The policy in several states is to forbid or discourage incorporation for college-related groups.

ACTIVITIES THAT NONPROFIT CORPORATIONS MAY NOT BE ALLOWED TO DO

State laws may explicitly deny certain activities for nonprofit incorporations. The list of forbidden actions varies from state to state, but here are areas that may be involved in your state:

1. The corporate name cannot be the same or deceptively similar to the name of another corporation.

2. The corporate name cannot contain any word or phrase that indicates or implies that the corporation is organized for any purpose other than those contained in its articles.

3. The corporation cannot make loans to its directors or officers.

4. The corporation cannot distribute any part of its income to its members, directors, or officers.

5. The corporation cannot pay dividends.

6. The corporation cannot issue shares of stock.

7. The corporation cannot acquire, hold, or dispose of funds and property for any unlawful purpose.

8. Directors of the corporation are individually liable for the misuse or misapplication of any money or funds through negligence.

9. Directors of the corporation must not be imprudent or careless in administering the affairs of the corporation.

10. Directors of the corporation may not willfully or otherwise violate the laws governing nonprofit corporations.

11. The corporation's official agent cannot have an address different from the corporation's office address.

12. The corporation cannot have an out-of-state resident serve as its official agent.

13. The corporation must avoid buying speculative stocks, especially those that produce no income.

14. The corporation may not be permitted to have members.

15. The corporation must dispose of gifts that are imprudent investments.

16. The corporation cannot refuse to incur debts to finance investments.

17. The corporation must avoid investment in land or buildings that do not pertain to its purposes or that do not produce income.

18. The corporation cannot use or divert its funds to pay for personal expenses.

19. The corporation must distribute its funds according to its purposes. It cannot fail to do so.

20. The corporation cannot pay excessive salaries or professional fees.

21. The corporation cannot sell its assets for less than fair market value.

22. The corporation cannot incur penalties (i.e., for building code violations, etc.).

23. The corporation must make trust property productive.

24. The corporation cannot leave excessive cash in non–income-producing bank accounts.

25. The corporation cannot incur federal taxes or penalties that could have been avoided.

26. The corporation cannot allow waste to incur.

27. A "foreign" (or out-of-state) corporation is not permitted to do business in a state unless it applies for and is granted "domestic" status.

28. Upon dissolution, the corporation cannot give its assets, or any part thereof, to its officers, directors, or members.

29. The corporation cannot buy or sell real or personal property unless such property deals directly with the corporation's purpose.

30. The words *engineering, bank, banking,* or *trust* cannot be used in the name of the corporation unless it is actually to be such an agency.

31. The corporation may not retain its charter it if fails to file its required annual report.

32. The directors, officers, and members cannot assume corporate powers without authorization.

33. The corporation cannot make investments that would jeopardize the purpose of the corporation.

34. It is not legally permissible in some states for a student publication in a public institution to incorporate.

35. The corporation cannot be capitalized at a level beyond that needed to achieve its purposes.

36. The corporation must distribute funds sufficient to avoid taxability.

37. The corporation cannot make taxable expenditures.

38. The corporation cannot retain "excess business holdings."

39. The corporation cannot engage in any act of self-dealing.

40. The corporation cannot be tax exempt if it participates in a political campaign, carries on propaganda, or attempts to influence legislation.

41. The corporation is not automatically eligible for tax-exempt status from federal income taxes.

42. The corporation is not automatically eligible for tax-exempt status from state taxes.

43. Gifts made to the corporation are not automatically eligible for deduction from the donors' state or federal income tax reports.

44. In some states, public institutions may not be permitted to allocate public funds in incorporated student publications. The current status of such rules should be checked since legislatures change laws yearly.

45. Corporations seeking federal income tax exemption must not engage in racially discriminatory practices, and they must proclaim through advertising and other means that they do not.

Each of these prohibitions should be checked carefully to be sure about its applicability in your state.

Unincorporated agencies, individuals, or organizations are virtually unaffected by any of these restraints.

TAX-EXEMPT STATUS

One of the most confusing and frustrating aspects of nonprofit corporations centers on tax exemption and liabilities. The fact that a corporation qualifies for nonprofit status does not mean that it automatically establishes tax-exempt status either on the federal or state level. The taxes involved could include income taxes, property taxes, sales taxes, or others.

The *Collegian* of Pennsylvania State University was clearly part of Penn State until the early 1970s when a contract was negotiated between *Collegian,* Inc., and the university. The newspaper's tax status started getting fuzzy at this point. The paper is still shielded by the university when it comes to tax matters. This shielding is more a matter of inertia than policy. The subject of the newspaper's tax status has been a perplexing problem for at least 10 years. The paper might qualify for a federal exemption under Internal Revenue Code 501(c)(3), but its state obligations remain unclear since the paper was turned down when it asked for exempt status as a charitable, educational, or religious institution.

Penn State recently stated that the *Collegian* was not part of the university. This statement means that the educational nature of the university cannot devolve on the newspaper.

Robert Tyron, revenue examiner for the Excise Tax Division of Iowa, indicates that the articles of incorporation establish that the *Iowa*

State Daily appears to be under the general administration of the university staff. Since the newspaper would thus be a part of the university, it would be granted the same sales tax exemption that the university has. The relation between the newspaper and its host university establishes the newspaper's educational status. The *Daily Iowan* of the University of Iowa is a nonprofit corporation exempt from both federal and state taxes.

Gerald H. Coy, general manager of the *State News,* serving Michigan State University, indicates that the newspaper is duly incorporated under the laws of Michigan as a nonprofit corporation and is exempt from all state and federal taxes, but the newspaper must submit to annual audits by state and federal revenue agents.

Obviously, advice about tax-exempt status is dangerous to provide since federal and state laws change markedly from year to year. A tax expert should be consulted to determine precisely what status a publication might qualify for.

If the student publication is fully independent of any host university on the basis of its articles of incorporation, that student publication cannot ride to tax exemption on the educational coattails of its host college. Instead it must fully and truthfully serve as an educational entity. It's not enough to say in the articles that the publication is dedicated to producing publications to educate readers. The education centers on the student staff who are learning newspapering. It is immaterial whether anyone reads the publication. A strong statement about educating students in the work of publishing must be included in the articles of incorporation. This might be insufficient if many of the staff are not students or if the relationships with the host institution are nebulous or nonexistent.

Tax-exempt status could become very important for a large publication that owns real estate and technical equipment upon which property or excise taxes can be levied. Sales tax on newsprint and other supply items could be a sizable amount. Although most publications seldom make measurable profits, they may not be excused from income tax. In some states, the state income tax is based on gross income, not net profits.

A problem of substance could also arise in that nonprofit corporations in many states and tax-exempt ones on the federal level are not supposed to engage in promoting political candidates or programs. Several years ago, the IRS gave the *Spectator* of Columbia University quite a bit of static on this point but backed away when public debate on the issue made the IRS appear a little silly. No such question has ever been raised by the IRS about student publications in public universities since IRS regulations for public and private institutions are very different.

Heavy revision of the federal income tax program may occur in any legislative year. Up-to-date IRS publications and consultation with tax experts are essential to determine tax status. In 1981, for example, the IRS noted that income generated from advertising sold by full-time employees could not qualify for tax-exempt status. State tax structures and laws may also change each year.

An incorporated and nonincorporated student publication that is part of a host university and participates in the educational purposes of that host university is exempt from the same state and federal taxes that the host university is exempted from.

According to *College and University Reports,* the IRS ruled that income generated by professional salespersons who sold advertising for an exempt college-oriented newspaper constitutes unrelated business taxable income because the activities were not substantially related to the organization's exempt purpose. In a letter ruling, the Internal Revenue Service said that the newspaper, although having no formal ties with a nearby university, was operated in conjunction with the university journalism curriculum and gave journalism students a form of on-the-job training. To generate advertising income sufficient to cover expenses, the newspaper hired professional advertising salespersons.

The IRS listed three conditions that must prevail before any activity is classified as an unrelated trade or business (under Internal Revenue Code Sec. 513) subject to tax. These are (1) the activity must be a trade or business; (2) the trade or business must be regularly carried on; and (3) the trade or business cannot be substantially related to exempt purposes; the business activity must be shown to have a substantial *causal* relationship to the accomplishment of the organization's exempt purpose.

The IRS held that to the extent that the newspaper utilized nonstudent employees, the advertising sales function did not have a substantial causal relationship to the educational purpose of providing training to student journalists. Therefore, income generated by such sales constituted taxable income (IRS Letter Ruling 8118049, February 6, 1981). Subsequently, some incorporated college newspapers were required to consider all advertising profits subject to income tax even if sold by students.

INCORPORATION—ADVANTAGES, DIFFICULTIES, AND RECOMMENDATIONS

Would incorporation as a nonprofit or profit-making corporation be of value to or advisable for student publications?

Here are some possible reasons why incorporation might be advantageous.

1. The publication, or group of publications, would become a separate legal entity.

2. A clear indication of the precise relationship of the student publication to the university can be provided in the articles of incorporation.

3. The articles of incorporation should clearly indicate that the university has no control and seeks no control over the content of the student publication.

4. The articles of incorporation should clearly designate the student editor as the one exercising free press rights.

5. The university may contract with the student publication for campuswide distribution sufficient to meet student interest. This contract would include payment by the university for copies provided.

6. The student publication could establish its own fiscal procedures, including the numbers and wages of full-time and part-time employees.

7. The publication could arrange lease-purchase plans for, or otherwise finance through loans, contemporary electronic equipment. (The cost of such equipment ranges from $50,000 to $250,000.)

8. The publication could employ competent management and legal counsel.

9. The publication might develop high morale and a sense of identity and mission.

10. Since the publication is incorporated, the university has no obligation for its debts or litigation.

11. Perhaps the most significant result of incorporation is the legal right to determine what to do with surplus earnings. Some institutions do not allow unincorporated publications to carry over surplus earnings, earn interest, spend money on travel, or plan long-range financial operation amortizing equipment purchases, and so on.

Here are some possible reasons that incorporation might cause serious difficulties.

1. The articles of incorporation may actually confuse or obscure the relationship of the student publication to the university.

2. The articles of incorporation can establish taboo subjects and place prohibitions on the content of student publications.

3. The articles of incorporation can require the student editor to submit materials for approval prior to publication to a manager named by the board of directors.

4. Universities could be tempted to discontinue any financial support arrangements for student publications.

5. Additional personnel and wages costs could impose financial problems for the publication.

6. Suppliers of equipment and other major items might be reluctant to do business with a corporation having few or unsure assets.

7. The cost of employing competent management could be prohibitive as could additional legal services. The number of full-time noneditorial personnel needed by an incorporated publication would probably be two or three more persons than needed by a nonincorporated publication.

8. The continuity of quality and effectiveness of the publication could become erratic and inconsistent as the endeavors of students and full-time managers fluctuate.

9. The cost of initial incorporation could be from $1,000 to $10,000.

10. The cost of maintaining a corporation could be from $1,000 to $20,000 each year.

11. The courts could determine that the university is truly obligated to pay the debts or litigation costs of an incorporated publication since the corporate veil does not sever the relationships or responsibilities.

What recommendations can be gathered from this report?

First, no publication or combination of publications on a single university campus should consider incorporation unless it has a gross income of about $500,000. In some instances a smaller operation might be successful if there are extenuating conditions, but only in a limited number of situations. The cost of operating a corporation could probably be absorbed in a $500,000 operation.

Second, the reason to incorporate student publications in public or state colleges is to enhance the editorial freedom of the student staff. However, case after case from the courts during the last 20 years has clearly established that administrators in state colleges cannot censor or otherwise control the content of student publications, incorporated or not.

Third, student publications in private colleges might be able to escape administrative censorship by incorporating, providing that the articles of incorporation strictly forbid administrative control.

Fourth, all of the advantages cited above for incorporation are readily attainable by nonincorporated publications. Almost all of the difficulties posed for incorporated publications can devolve upon unincorporated publications. On balance, it seems that incorporation may or may not deliver very much.

Fifth, both incorporated and unincorporated publications need skillful management, competent advisers, and hardworking students who respect the integrity and nature of each publication.

Sixth, the university, committed to the inquiring mind and the development of the intelligent human being, should cherish and sustain a free student campus press and even defend such a press from its detractors on or off campus. This should be true whether the student publication is incorporated or unincorporated.

Seventh, if the only way a student publication can escape a domineering administration would be to incorporate as a profit-making unit and move off campus, consideration of such a plan might be justified, especially in representative private colleges. Not many have done so or are presently planning such a move.

Eighth, no move toward incorporation should be undertaken until a careful analysis of restraints and requirements can be made in the state where the college is located.

Ninth, it seems doubtful that incorporation should seriously be contemplated for 200 campuses across the land because of costs and legal problems.

Tenth, not-for-profit incorporation might enhance the possibility of obtaining FCC licensing of student-operated FM radio stations.

Incorporation is no panacea to right wrongs or solve problems. It could pose even greater difficulties. What is really needed is a situation wherein student publications are adequately and stably financed and have assurance that editorial censorship or recrimination will not be imposed. If competent advisers are available and intelligent students participate, the resulting lively student publication will be a joy to read, a goal to honor, a criterion of learning, and a cauldron of debate.

CERTAIN LEGAL IMPLICATIONS OF OPERATING A NOT-FOR-PROFIT CORPORATION TO PUBLISH A STUDENT NEWSPAPER

(At the suggestion of the American Bar Association, College Media Advisers asked attorney Richard E. Deer, of the Barnes, Hickham, Pantzer and Boyd law firm, Indianapolis, Indiana, to evaluate incorporation provisions for student publications generally. Deer and his associate Douglas Long prepared this report for CMA, which should prove of great value to any student publication staff contemplating incorporation.)

Many of the student newspapers published at colleges and universities in the United States are not owned and operated by not-for-profit corporations. Many of these newspapers are published by entities which are not incorporated. For many reasons, those who manage a business which publishes a student newspaper in unincorporated form may wish to change the form in which their business is operated by establishing a not-for-profit corporation. This memorandum discusses certain of the legal implications of operating a not-for-profit corporation to publish a student newspaper.

The legal implications herein discussed are divided into two categories — those pertaining to the establishment and maintenance of the business as a not-for-profit corporation and those pertaining to securing an exemption from federal income tax liability. The legal implications of establishing and maintaining such a not-for-profit corporation will be discussed first.

A. Certain Corporate Legal Implications of Establishing and Maintaining a Not-For-Profit Corporation to Publish a Student Newspaper

1. Powers

The laws of many states permit domestic not-for-profit corporations to exercise broad powers. The law in Indiana, for example, recognizes that a not-for-profit corporation incorporated in Indiana generally will have, subject to any limitations imposed by the corporation's articles of incorporation, such powers and rights as to continue in existence perpetually, to sue and be sued in its corporate name, to acquire, utilize and dispose of property, to borrow money, to issue, sell or pledge its obligations, to transact business outside of Indiana, to appoint officers and agents, [and] to do acts which are necessary, convenient or expedient to carry out the purposes for which the corporation was formed.[2] Similar powers are granted not-for-profit corporations incorporated under the law of Ohio.[3] Thus, the laws of many states permit a domestic not-for-profit corporation to publish a student newspaper.

2. Articles of Incorporation or Charter

Generally, in incorporating a business which publishes a student newspaper, articles of incorporation or a charter must be filed with the office of the Secretary of State of the state in which the incorporation is to be made. The statutes of many states prescribe that certain information must be included in the articles of incorporation or charter of a domestic not-for-profit corporation. An Indiana statute, for example, prescribes that the articles of incorporation of a domestic not-for-profit corporation must set forth: (1) the name of the corporation, (2) the purpose or purposes for which it is formed, (3) the period of time during which it is to continue as a corporation, if the time is to be limited, (4) the post-office address of its principal office and the name and address of its resident agent, (5) a description of the classes of members and a statement of the relative rights of each class, (6) the number of directors constituting the initial board of directors, (7) the names and addresses of the first board of directors, (8) the names and addresses of the incorporators, and (9) a statement of the property and an estimate of its value, to be taken over by the corporation upon its incorporation.[4] A Kentucky statute prescribes that information similar to that described above be included in the articles of incorporation of a not-for-profit corporation incorporated under the laws of Kentucky.[5]

3. By-Laws

In addition to mandating the filing of articles of incorporation or of a charter, the laws of many states permit a domestic not-for-profit corporation to adopt by-laws. Under Indiana law, an Indiana not-for-profit corporation is permitted to adopt by-laws.[6] Such by-laws "may contain any provision for the regulation and management of the affairs of the corporation" not inconsistent with the articles of incorporation or the laws of Indiana.[7] Thus, the by-laws of an Indiana not-for-profit corporation publishing a student newspaper could include provisions respecting the time and place of holding and the manner of conducting meetings of members, the manner of calling special meetings of directors or members, the powers, duties, tenure and qualifications of officers and directors of the corporation and the time, place, and manner of electing them.[8] The laws of Kentucky and Ohio also contemplate the adoption of by-laws by domestic not-for-profit corporations.[9] In short, guiding legal principles for the operation and maintenance of a student newspaper business generally could be included in the by-laws and articles of incorporation or charter of a particular not-for-profit corporation so that the student newspaper business could be operated in such corporate form.

4. Special Powers

Of the many legal problems which may arise when a student newspaper is published by a not-for-profit corporation, three bear noting. First, under certain circumstances, a court may refuse to recognize as a not-for-profit corporation an entity which is so styled. If the initial capitalization of such a non-profit "corporation" is not adequate to cover the reasonably foreseeable risks of publishing a student newspaper, a court might "pierce the corporate veil" and find the members of the "corporation" personally liable.[10] Moreover, if the not-for-profit corporation was operated in such a manner that corporate formalities such as keeping corporate records and segregating corporate funds from other funds were disregarded, a court might also disregard the corporate entity and treat the publication of the student newspaper as an unincorporated business.[11]

Second, the laws of many states require a domestic not-for-profit corporation to make annual administrative filings. Not-for-profit corporations incorporated in Indiana, or Kentucky, for example, are required to file an annual report with the office of the appropriate Secretary of State each year.[12] In addition, informational or actual state tax returns may be required. Thus, operating a student newspaper in corporate form entails administrative costs.

Finally, those who operate a student newspaper as a not-for-profit corporation, although legally independent of the educational institution upon which they report, will not become, by means of incorporating alone, invulnerable to pressure imposed upon them by the institution to adopt editorial or reporting positions or policies.

5. Advantages and Disadvantages of Operating as a Not-For-Profit Corporation

The publication of a student newspaper using a not-for-profit corporate form of organization has advantages and disadvantages. Only a few of the principal advantages and disadvantages will be noted here. Among the principal advantages of operating in such form are: (1) the business entity can possess a perpetual existence; and (2) the liability for corporate debts of the share-holders or members of the not-for-profit corporation in normal circumstances will be limited to their investments. The principal disadvantages of utilizing such corporate form include: (1) the administrative costs of making required filings; and (2) to establish and maintain the good standing of the corporation, the costly aid of lawyers and certified public accountants probably will be required.

B. Certain Tax Implications of Establishing and Operating a Not-For-Profit Corporation to Publish a Student Newspaper

Section 501(a) of the Internal Revenue Code (the "Code") provides that certain organizations identified in Code sections 501(c), 501(d) and 401(a) are exempt from federal income taxation. Code Section 501(c)(3) states that such exempt organizations include "corporations . . . organized and operated exclusively for religious, charitable, scientific, testing for public safety, literary or educational purposes . . ." A not-for-profit corporation which publishes a student newspaper may qualify for exemption from federal income taxation as a corporation organized and operated exclusively for literary and-or educational purposes within the meaning of Code 501.

Generally, to obtain recognition for exemption from federal income taxation, it is advisable for the not-for-profit corporation to file an application for exempt status with the Internal Revenue Service.[13] Form 1023, entitled *Application for Recognition of Exemption Under Section 501(c)(3)*

of the Internal Revenue Code, is a form specifically prescribed by the Internal Revenue Service (the "Service") which may be used by such a not-for-profit corporation.[14] Filing articles of incorporation and establishing a not-for-profit corporate form of organization will not alone qualify an organization for exemption from federal income taxation. The tax-exempt status of an educational institution upon which a student newspaper business operating in not-for-profit corporate form exists, likewise will not alone make the not-for-profit corporation exempt from federal income taxation.

Form 1023 calls for a great variety of information about the applying corporation's actual proposed capitalization, activities, purposes and operations. A ruling or determination letter will be issued to the not-for-profit corporation if its application and accompanying documents demonstrate that the corporation is an organization of the type described in 501(c)(3).[15] Should the student publication business wish to secure 501(c)(3) status prior to incorporating, the business may apply for such status before incorporating. The Service will issue a ruling or determination letter favorable to the applicant in advance of incorporation if the proposed conclusion is that the organization will qualify under 501 (c)(3).[16]

Even though a not-for-profit corporation is qualified as tax exempt from federal income taxation, it still may be liable for tax on its unrelated business taxable income. Unrelated business taxable income is defined as the gross income derived from any unrelated trade or business regularly carried on less certain deductions which are directly connected with the carrying on of such trade or business.[17] An unrelated trade or business is a trade or business the conduct of which is not substantially related to the exercise or performance by the organization of the purpose or function constituting the basis for its exemption under Code 501.[18] Moreover, even if a not-for-profit corporation would qualify under 501(c)(3) and would have no unrelated business taxable income, the corporation probably would still be required to file with the Service an annual information return on Form 990.[19]

Under the laws of many states, many not-for-profit corporations, particularly those operated for charitable, religious, or educational purposes, are exempt from most, if not all, state and local taxes.[20] In many cases, a not-for-profit corporation will be required to establish affirmatively its right to exemption for the appropriate state authority. The laws of several states prescribing conditions for exemptions from tax are very similar to 501(c)(3).[21] Thus, in several states, a domiciliary not-for-profit corporation which published a student newspaper and which had qualified for exemption from federal income taxation could also qualify for exemption from some, if not all, of the taxes imposed by its state of domicile. In those states in which exemption provisions in state statutes are very similar to 501(c)(3), an exemption from federal income taxation under 501 would be persuasive, if not conclusive, evidence that the organization is entitled to an exemption from some, or all, state taxes.

Conclusion

The laws of many states permit a not-for-profit corporation to carry on the business of publishing a student newspaper. Under the laws of many states articles of incorporation or a charter must be filed with the appropriate state authority before a not-for-profit corporation can be legally established. With the articles or charter, the by-laws of a not-for-profit corporation may be used to furnish guidelines by which the not-for-profit corporation can be operated.

Organizing a not-for-profit corporation to publish a student newspaper, while in normal circumstances affording limited liability to the corporation's shareholders or members, is not without cost. Maintaining corporate formalities to safeguard against the piercing of the corporate veil, resolving legal and accounting problems which would probably arise and making necessary administrative filings would all be costly tasks.

If a not-for-profit corporation publishing a student newspaper was established and operated exclusively for a literary and/or educational purpose, the corporation would have a good chance of qualifying as a 501(c)(3) organization generally exempt from federal income taxation. The organization might also qualify as exempt from some, if not all, of the state and local taxes to which it otherwise would be subject. Even in the event of such qualification, however, the generation of business income not related to the corporation's literary and educational purposes could result in the imposition of federal and state income tax liability.

CHAPTER 6

Publisher

Perhaps no more confusion is found in the field of college student publications than in understanding the word *publisher.* In data collected by College Media Advisers, this confusion appeared in answers provided by college officials when they were asked what agency was considered the publisher of the college newspaper:

254, the college or university
162, student government
 71, a publications board or committee
 66, the board of trustees
 51, confused publishing with printing
 44, no campus papers
 41, a corporation
 38, no answer
 33, students
 29, the student staff of the newspaper
 26, the journalism department or a journalism class
 25, the president (or chancellor)
 20, no one
 13, the student personnel area
  9, public relations officers
  4, in doubt
  4, avoided the question by reporting they were closing down
  2, a universitywide senate
  1, each of these agencies: the English department, the state of Wisconsin, a college-community council, a campus affairs commission, the office of student publications

When the colleges were asked to cite a state law establishing the legality of the publishing agency, only 53 reported there was such a law, they believed. But 698 said there was no such law, and another 93 did not answer. Six colleges based their system on opinions of state attorneys' offices, and nine believed the university charter established the authority. The board of trustees in 21 colleges authorized the plan, while 19 relied on state nonprofit corporation laws.

More curious answers were reported when the college officials were asked to name the individual who served as the publisher for the campus newspaper. The answers: in 678 colleges and universities no one was publisher; 95 colleges failed to answer. Thirty-five indicated a journalism teacher or adviser was the publisher; 35 decided the student editor was the publisher. Thirty-four named the college president; 12 named various college officials; and 7 thought one of their public relations officers was the publisher. Other persons mentioned included the student government president, an editorial board, or the student government.

Yearbooks didn't fare much differently than newspapers. The *publishing agency* cited most often (193 times) was the college. Student government was next at 128. As for the rest:

57 colleges confused *publishing* with *printing*
54, a publications committee
38, the board of trustees
34, no one
31, the student staff
18, the student personnel area
18, students
14, a corporation
11, the journalism department or classes
11, the college president
 8, a public relations office
 5, the yearbook editor
 4, the senior class

Also mentioned were upperclass students, New Jersey, and the business department.

As for laws establishing their publishing agency, 588 colleges knew of none, while 24 said there was a legal basis.

As for naming an *individual* serving as the publisher, 562 colleges reported none. Mentioned most often as publisher were the editor of the yearbook (24), the yearbook adviser (19), and the president (17).

Also mentioned were a vice president, the student personnel area, and the graphic arts head. Two colleges confused printing with publishing.

If incorporation and/or independence are helpful in organizing student publications, the universities having such a plan should be knowledgeable about publishers. But here are answers from such colleges:

41 newspapers indicated the publishing agency was a corporation
10, students
 3, a publications board or committee
 2, no one
 2, no information

Also mentioned were the university, the president, and a private company.

14 yearbooks named a corporation
 4, the student government
 3, the student staff
 3, no one
 3, students
 2, the editor

Thirty incorporated independent newspapers and 19 such yearbooks reported that no laws authorized their status. Nineteen newspapers believed the nonprofit corporation laws provided authority, and one newspaper indicated a state law applied. Seven colleges reported state laws covering yearbooks, and four colleges said board of trustees' regulations covered newspapers.

The clarity with which corporate independent publications operate becomes somewhat clouded when 39 colleges report that no one serves as the publisher of the newspaper and 26 colleges say no one serves as publisher of the yearbook. One yearbook publisher was said to be the editor, and one was the adviser. Six editors and six college officials were named as publishers of newspapers, and an editorial board and the student government were also mentioned.

The word *publisher* is a generally misunderstood term. Although a college could be considered a publishing agency, it could not properly be called a publisher. A publisher is an individual who performs management functions for the owners of the publishing company or agency.

Colleges generally have not designated anyone to perform these functions. If no one has such a function, whether that person be a student or a college official, it should not be surprising that confusion often accompanies the operation of student publications. In any case, the so-called independent, incorporated publications apparently were not any better organized or more knowledgeable on this score than other student publications.

Courts have constantly ruled that a state college or its agents cannot be considered the publisher of a student publication because they cannot control the content of the publication as the publisher of a commercial publication does. The First Amendment forbids federal officials or agencies from control. The Fourteenth Amendment forbids state, municipal, or other government officials or agencies from control. This has been the attitude of the courts since the 1925 *Gitlow* decision. Since the *student staff* controls the content of the publication, it, in effect, under the leadership of the student editor, serves as publisher, even if university personnel provide advice, technical help, or financial assistance.

CHAPTER 7

Censorship

Censorship of the campus press could be accomplished only if someone other than the student staff
was in a position to approve copy prior to publication. A College Media Advisers study attempted to
determine how widespread such a practice might be, in light of the
contentions of the mythmakers that it surely was universal.

Reports submitted by college officials indicated that no one approved student newspaper copy prior to publication on 498 campuses.

An examination of the 39 percent where prior approval was practiced bears some explanation. In 273 colleges, the adviser of the newspaper gave prior approval; in 43 cases, other persons did so. Advisers
generally checked copy for libel, good taste, or legal matters but did
not forbid publication of ideas or viewpoints critical of the university.
In 42 cases, the prior approval system was very weak.

The campus yearbook staff did not have to seek prior approval in
351 colleges, but did in 264 colleges. Thus, no prior approval was
involved in 57 percent of the colleges. In 243 of the colleges, the adviser
of the yearbook gave prior approval; the yearbook staff had to obtain
approval from other persons in 7 cases. Once again, the level of approval was not necessarily severe; indeed, in 13 colleges it was very
weak.

Courts at every level simply do not tolerate discipline or censorship
against the campus press by state college officials. A heavy dossier of
cases is building up to indicate that censorship is illegal in state colleges.

The U.S. Supreme Court has not handled cases involving student
press freedom issues to any great extent. Its ruling in the 1973 *Papish*
case was a landmark decision favoring student publishing efforts in

state colleges. The Court has subsequently refused to hear appeals in three cases. U.S. courts of appeal have produced at least 11 pro-student free press decisions, and federal district courts have upheld student publications in state colleges at least a dozen times. Thus, in the federal court system student publications in state colleges have won 24 favorable judgments denying censorship power to university officials.

State court systems have favored student publications in state colleges at least 15 times and actually ruled only once against a student publication. Students in private colleges have rarely gone to court to seek protection from censorship. By midcentury they had lost three cases, but in the last few years they have won three times. One other case saw a student obtain a handsome out-of-court settlement from her college.

Details about these cases can be found in *Freedom for the College Student Press,* by Louis E. Ingelhart, published by Greenwood Press (1985). Additional and updated information can be found in the *Report* provided (three times per year) by the Student Press Law Center in Washington, D.C. Persons should be cautioned not to consider cases involving high school publications as having any effect on the college student press. Courts consistently treat the high school press very differently because of the supposed immaturity of such pupils. The effect of the Twenty-sixth Amendment has been to make all college students adults and thus too sophisticated for the supposedly redemptive functions of censorship.

Herman Estrin, a past president of College Media Advisers active in advising college publications at Newark College of Engineering in New Jersey, spent several months reading issues of 200 college newspapers and concluded at the end of his study that "the collegiate press in the 1970s was producing a forthright, candid approach to the real problems, concerns, and interests of its readers—the student body. College editors—responsible, sophisticated, knowledgeable, provocative, and at times, irreverent and daring—offered their readers an informative, stimulating, timely press."

The commercial press would appreciate such an accolade. Estrin found a wide range of concerns published in the papers. The college press, like the commercial press, was able to tackle anything.

If censorship was widely practiced on the campus press, student newspapers could not have written about this list of subjects Estrin read about repeatedly:

1. Commitment to service activities designed to improve the community and help needy persons in the off-campus community.

2. Sex was treated casually, frankly, and relevantly with articles about centers for human sexuality, sex forums, birth control, abortion, homosexuality, marriage, family planning, venereal disease, cohabitation, and rape.

3. In the advertisement sections, students included such ads as abortion information and assistance, male contraceptives, Alcoholics Anonymous, narcotic addicts rehabilitation, GROPE (Gay Rights of People Everywhere), Tampax tampons, term papers researched and professionally typed, draft counseling, and pregnancy counseling.

4. The college press was definitely concerned about the thefts, assaults, vandalism, and murders on campus.

5. Evaluation of faculty effectiveness by students.

6. Jobs.

7. Student editors spoke out against the war in Vietnam and deplored its continuance.

8. Revision of the curriculum to include timely and relevant courses.

9. Campus newspapers championed students' rights and the rights of others.

10. Some papers presented an entire supplement, "The Arts." However, most papers had a single page devoted to the arts. Students wrote reviews expressing reactions to the latest records, provocative motion pictures, operas, ballets, books, concerts, television, radio attractions, and even belly dancing.

11. Many papers offered counseling services, which included personal, vocational, alcoholic, medical, drug, academic, sexual, draft, and term paper counseling.

12. Students advanced their ideas concerning the economy and discussed noise and water pollution, recycling, food facts, food fraud, herbicides, and soil and beach erosion.

13. Women's liberation.

14. The use of obscenities in campus newspapers declined. Most upset by their use was the faculty, not the students. Many editors admitted that the obscenities had lost their shock value. Others claimed that the use of obscenities in the collegiate press indicated immaturity in the writer.

15. In addition to these popular concerns of the collegiate press, college newspapers wrote about more effective teaching, tenure of professors, salaries of staff and professors, parking problems, pass-fail grades, the "new religion," and students' participation in curriculum planning and in-college governance.[1]

Most of the above information pertained to public colleges. This does not mean that private colleges can censor with no restraint. Freedom of the press is a right guaranteed to individuals. The key individual in college press matters is the editor. Not many cases involving private college students have worked through the courts yet, however.

But judgment should prevail. Officials at Brigham Young University concluded that its student editors have essentially the same rights as do editors in public colleges. Many private colleges are proud of the campus traditions of free inquiry and discussion. They proclaim in university policies their endorsement of a free press.

It is good advice to a college administrator not to take action against the student press, even though the press has been obnoxious or severe. The danger is not only in court action but also in on-campus relations.

Here is a plaintive report concerning the *Fourth Estate* of Hilbert College in 1971:

The editor in chief of the Hilbert College (Hamburg, N.Y.) student newspaper was cleared of charges of "breach of trust" brought against him for running a Planned Parenthood advertisement.

Dan Hickling, a freshman at the two-year coeducational college, was found not guilty of charges leveled by President Sister May Edwina Bogel.

Three weeks earlier Hilbert's *Fourth Estate* had run a large back-page ad that read in part: "Get to know how the two of you don't have to become the three of you. Or the four of you. Planned Parenthood. Children by choice. Not chance." The ad, a public service announcement by the National Advertising Council, quoted statistics saying that "more than half of all pregnancies each year are accidental."

Sister May Edwina called Mr. Hickling into her office and told him he faced expulsion from school if he did not print an apology for running the ad. He refused. Sister May Edwina told Mr. Hickling the ad was an "attack on the Catholic church." She said it was a direct contradiction to the pope's encyclical against birth control and could not appear in a paper bearing the college's name.

Mr. Hickling defended the ad on the grounds that his primary obligation was to the students and not the church. He told Sister May Edwina, "I have done nothing wrong."

Following the meeting, Sister May Edwina filed a written charge that led to the hearing. She charged that the Planned Parenthood ad "is unacceptable to Catholic tenets and undermines the authentic values of the faith."

She added that "when interrogated whether he [Mr. Hickling] was aware that this advertisement was contrary to the teaching of the church, he replied that he was . . . but he had an obligation as an editor in chief to inform the public.

"This is a breach of trust on the part of the editor in chief. This was an improper use of the college newspaper. He has shown no respect for Catholic philosophy and morals and disregarded the aims of the college. He has failed in his responsibility to God and fellow students and the founders of this college.

"The college reserves the right to prohibit attacks on the Catholic faith. Every individual on this campus must respect the right of religious freedom and that no attacks against the Catholic faith openly or by innuendo will be tolerated."

A seven-member panel — four students, two faculty members, and Sister May Edwina's top assistant — heard Mr. Hickling and Sister May Edwina, and discussed the charges for two hours. The hearing was closed; however, Mr. Hickling was entitled to the aid of counsel and was represented by Steve Lipman, student affairs editor.

The unanimous 7–0 decision: "Mr. Hickling shall *not* be expelled from school. He shall *not* be removed as editor in chief. A list of guidelines pertaining to the relationship between the editor in chief and the newspaper's adviser shall be drawn up." It was suggested that the adviser's role be limited to determining libel, not editorial comment.

The Student Press Law Center of Washington, D.C., issues a magazine-style report three times each year that contains discussions of public and private college efforts to censor, restrain, chill, or punish student expression in student publications. It would be pleasant to indicate such episodes are diminishing, but they have remained at the same level for several decades. Censorship seemingly occurs in cycles across the nation. Student journalists in public colleges have gone to court from time to time to seek redress. They have won several cases and lost very few.

Censorship, or prior restraint of copy for the campus press, is not the standard procedure practiced in most American colleges and universities, public or private. Perhaps the incidence is higher than it should be; much of the purpose of studies such as this one is to advise college administrators to recognize the desirability of a free and uncensored campus press. College Media Advisers, Inc., suggests endorsement and understanding of the function of a free campus press.

Administrative attitudes toward censoring student publications by various control techniques swing on a pendulum of inexperience. Some administrators have short longevity; newcomers are apt to make control mistakes. The common scheme is to threaten to reduce or eliminate funding or facilities. Student governments, student personnel people, presidents, and deans have been known to use this ploy in a heavy-handed manner. Another plan is to assign grievance power to a publications board or committee to exert content pressure either to chill or control content. This was a frequent move in the 1980s. Firing the editor, kicking the publication off campus, making the publication a controlled classroom activity—all are devices. They do not work well or for any length of time. Repression is the surest way to inspire college students to turn to scurrilous underground publications. Threatening or imposing punishments is legally and pedagogically ineffective.

College administrators contemplating such actions would be well advised to read the court cases about freedom of the student press and its funding. The impact of both the First and Fourteenth Amendments should be fully understood.

Advice before and criticism after publication by an adviser or other persons are not restraints, but are part of the learning process of a student journalist and a student publication.

Continuing studies by CMA and other agencies indicate that about two-thirds of the student publications in state colleges and more than half in private colleges operate in an atmosphere of freedom where the student staff is able to publish what it pleases without prior restraint, prior review, censorship, or punishment. This commitment to free expression fluctuates from year to year, but the level remains fairly constant.

In 1990 and 1991, hundreds of colleges and universities developed speech codes in efforts to reduce racial and ethnic clashes on their campuses. These codes were not able to be sustained in court actions because they violated the First Amendment free speech provision in state institutions. Whether continuing efforts to restrain speech on campuses will impact on the student press is not yet clear.

CHAPTER 8

Troubles in
the Courts

In almost every discussion of the student press, the term *libel* usually surfaces very early (others are *invasion of privacy, obscenity,* and *copyright violation*). Voices thin to fearful whispers as if libel were the devil incarnate to the printed word. For many years, libel has been used sincerely or falsely as a reason for the student press not to publish many things. Discussions by the mythmakers, including ill-informed boards of publications and some college administrators, all present a view of libel thus: Remarks that are critical of and unfair to people are surely uncalled-for and constitute a form of libel. If they are published, the resources of the university can be depleted by resulting lawsuits, which will surely end in five- or six-figure damages. If the university or college is not thus impoverished, surely the board, the president, and other administrative officials will have to pay personally.

Does libel work this way? Not at all.

Libel, of course, is visual defamation. Articles that hold persons up to public hatred, ridicule, or scorn and have the effect of destroying professional reputations can be said to be libelous. Libel as it is printed by newspapers is a civil matter, not a criminal one. This means that there is no agency that exercises surveillance over the contents of newspapers to determine if someone should be prosecuted for destroying a reputation. A court can consider a libel action only when a person who believes he has been legally abused under the terms of a state's civil defamation laws seeks to recover money damages to compensate for that abuse.

Not all things that can be embarrassing or critical are actionable in a libel case, however. In tort procedure, the court must first determine that the alleged libel was published. Second, the court determines that the material pertained to the person entering the suit. Third, the court determines whether the material is actually libelous. But no damages are assessed at this point. Instead, the court asks if the journalist has a legal justification for having printed the material. Legal justifications include truth, qualified privilege, or comment and criticism. There is no federal libel law so these cases are initiated in state courts.

The U.S. Supreme Court's 1964 *New York Times* v. *Sullivan* decision provides a federal or First Amendment defense against civil suits brought by *public officials* or public figures, who are required to prove the published material is actually false or was published with reckless disregard of the truth or actual malice. In 1986 the Supreme Court ruled that *private individuals* also had to prove the falsity of published material in defamation actions against newspapers. The states have statutory laws, and each state is apt to be different from the others in some way. Federal appellate courts, including the Supreme Court, have had to measure these varying state laws against the superior law of the Constitution.

A series of court decisions have now made it very difficult for anyone to sue a newspaper for libel successfully. The total effect of libel laws and court decisions is heavily weighted to protect the press more than the plaintiff. College newspapers have no less advantage than commercial newspapers in libel matters.

During the 50 years before 1985, the record of successful libel suits against college student publications was very sparse. Indeed, there appear to have been only a few such judgments. One awarded $1,900; a second provided only $10 to the plaintiff. There were, however, out-of-court settlements provided to litigants by universities and publications. The largest settlements were for $50,000 by the *Michigan State News,* which was covered by libel insurance, and $50,000 by Western Michigan University, also covered by liability insurance.

Student publications won 29 cases because courts ruled no actionable libel had occurred. In 1989 there were about 10 cases still in the courts or otherwise unresolved. One of these was for $80 million, filed against a literary magazine by a Santa Clara alumnus offended by a discussion of his support of the college's intercollegiate athletic program. Usually the amounts sought are astronomical but are reduced to quite small out-of-court settlements or eliminated altogether by the courts. A report indicates the $80 million case never proceeded. Of the 60 cases that have been recorded, 10 have involved student publications other than newspapers. Half of the newspaper cases have involved incorporated student newspapers.

When the total amount expended to pay for libel judgments or out-of-court settlements is added up, that sum does not equal one judgment made against a faculty member. A student won $200,000 from the head of the chemistry department who had libeled him.

Compared to the commercial press, the college press has a very superior record. This does not mean, of course, that either is libel-free. Perhaps professors and students are really such good friends of the campus press that they wouldn't consider filing libel suits. Many advisers reported that their publications had been threatened by a suit, but nothing happened. Probably the irritated persons got cold feet or found from legal counsel that the published matter was in no way actionable. Most of these advisers felt the threats weren't really serious.

Retractions were frequently published. Many advisers reported that student papers had provided retractions; of these, two-thirds said the student journalists took the initiative to correct errors, while only one-third of the advisers said the retractions were printed because of libel suit possibility.

In addition to the classic defenses against libel, educational institutions have two other avenues to escape liability. One is the doctrine of *charitable immunity,* which may protect private (and nonprofit) colleges from liability. If libel suits are contemplated against private colleges in states where charitable immunity is recognized, courts will readily refuse to sustain the suit. The doctrine of *governmental immunity,* based on the Eleventh Amendment, extends to public colleges. At least 11 states have terminated governmental immunity, however. Another legal doctrine is *agency law.* If a person acts outside the scope of his employment, his supervisors and advisers may not be held liable. Legal counsel would certainly have to evaluate the applicability of these doctrines in specific instances.

The courts have ruled that a state university is not liable for libelous content if it or its agents or officers do not control that content. If, however, any agent or officer of the state university does affect or control content, then the state university becomes fully liable.

From a legal theory approach and a review of actual case histories it becomes clear that libel (or losses therefrom) in student publications does not pose a threat to universities or student journalists who know what they are doing.

There have been only eight invasion of privacy cases involving student publications. The plaintiffs won four limited out-of-court settlements, but the courts exonerated the student publications in the remaining four. Copyright violations by student publications rarely reach the courts. Charles Schultz and United Features have won cases against college student publications and other college agencies in efforts to protect the integrity of the *Peanuts* characters. Usually they do not seek money awards. The *Superman* people went to court to force a community college not to call its newspaper the *Daley Planet,* but their fuss ended in an out-of-court agreement.

Apparently, alleged obscenity in college student publications is only a fearful reaction to poor taste. In the six cases in which obscenity was an issue, the courts found in favor of the student publications. There have been no obscenity convictions for college journalists.

When a case is settled out of court, the plaintiff usually accepts a limited sum, agrees never to reenter the case, and admits that the publication has not acted improperly in its publication of material.

An examination of decisions made in courts throughout the United States indicates that administrators of public colleges and universities may not exercise prior restraint or censorship of student publications. Courts have not fully addressed this issue for private institutions. College officials in state institutions may refuse distribution on campus of publications posing a real and severe threat of disruption or danger to people or property, but they cannot exert any control over the distribution of such publications off campus. Officials may establish reasonable regulations covering the time, place, and manner of distribution of any publications, including student publications, providing the regulations are clear and are applied with fairness to all publications.

The courts have not established authority for these college officials to restrain, forbid, or punish for libelous or obscene material. Both libel and obscenity are complex legal matters. Only the person libeled has any recourse for such material; state agencies have no role to play in seeking damages for libel. And obscenity must await a judicial determination of its existence before action can be taken through criminal proceedings.

College officials are wary of lawsuits based on libel or other content matters. Very few such lawsuits are based upon content in student publications. No more than two or three surface each year among the thousands of student publications of the nation's 3,600 colleges. Unfortunately, persons or agencies other than those associated with student publications become involved in litigation concerning libelous matter or actions. Most colleges find they must retain or staff legal counsel to handle such matters. This situation calls for rather heavy expenditures and budgeting. It is no wonder that colleges are hypersensitive about litigation. But they are looking in the wrong places when they list student publications as a litigation problem area. They would be better advised to conduct workshops for administrators or faculty members about how to avoid libel.

CHAPTER 9

Journalism Education

The academic success story of the 1970s and 1980s has been the discipline of journalism. Enrollments in existing programs grew remarkably, but the rapid establishment of new journalism programs in many colleges became a phenomenon. Colleges, eager to compete for larger enrollments, expanded curricular offerings greatly. Journalism became a most promising area since it attracted many young people and became important in the general or liberal arts concepts of many colleges.

By the mid-1980s more than 300 four-year colleges offered a journalism major, and many two-year colleges had extensive programs. Many more institutions provided a journalism minor, and it became rather standard for others to offer a course or two. Much of this increase was inspired by colleges seeking to provide learning opportunities for students to improve their student publications.

The approach was based upon the belief that if enough students took enough well-taught journalism courses and a well-qualified adviser was available to counsel student staff members and provide continuity, the student publications would improve and serve their readers well. Under such circumstances, worry about content in student publications simply evaporated.

Journalism education became caught up in the academic mazes that have created much confusion about higher education. Journalism is still going through the cauliflowerization, with its new important-sounding names such as communications, mass communications, communications research, communications theory, communications sociology, or journalism specialization skills.

One view of journalism education is that it is professional education. Another is that it is the most liberal of the liberal arts. Another, that it is now a theory-oriented area. Another, that it is a research discipline. It is now in the midst of new media relationships, computers, and other astonishing technologies.

The most vigorous of the agencies defining journalism education is the American Council for Education in Journalism and Mass Communications, which has accredited journalism in about one-third of the colleges offering journalism-major programs. It emphasizes professionalism, research, and theory but does not accept fully, as many colleges do, the liberal arts nature of journalism study. It insists that journalism students earn at least 60 semester hours of nonjournalism liberal arts course work and 30 additional hours of nonjournalism courses. Ideally, undergraduate journalism majors should earn only one-fourth of their academic credit in journalism courses.

In some institutions having large journalism programs, those departments have abandoned student publications. They thus avoid blame for what the student publications publish, worry about free press practicalities or philosophies, financial or legal liabilities, time drained from the required delights of research or theory, and student interference with publish-or-perish pressures. They resent the accusations of critics who consider their journalism program to be mere vocational training or perhaps unnecessary.

Most colleges having either small or large journalism programs, however, endorse the student publications, encourage them, and provide faculty advisers who function essentially as teachers and protect student staff from censorship, restraints, or punishments. The student publications are an essential part of the journalism program because they provide significant laboratory opportunities and other learning experiences.

This student publications laboratory, informal as it may be, is generally preferred over the sterile in-class laboratory newspaper some colleges find they must maintain, staff, and finance.

The Newspaper Fund, maintained by Dow-Jones, has reported that more than 90 percent of the college journalism graduates hired by American daily newspapers have earned their professional appointments as a direct result of significant staff experience on student newspapers.

Journalism is a broad term encompassing all aspects of print media and most aspects of electronic media as well as theoretical and philosophical bases of such media and their impact on society. This makes for a complex education package.

Journalism education is somewhat more expensive than some disciplines because writing and editing classes should be small (15 students) and laboratories replete with printing and electronic equipment are necessary. Publishing or broadcasting is frequently involved.

A few colleges have decided that journalism is such a high-level professional and academic area that it should be offered only at graduate levels. A few colleges restrict undergraduate journalism study to the junior and senior years. Most four-year colleges allow freshmen to take some courses and stretch the journalism curriculum over four years. Several community colleges have extensive offerings.

Vigorous debates over which is best and who should do what in journalism education keep this complex field in turmoil.

No person should be more aware of the reason for and the desirability of a free campus press than a journalism teacher. Journalism teacher-advisers need to be made of strong fiber to withstand the harassment of colleagues and superiors. They are generally tempered in the campus crucible.

Journalism is concerned at the moment communication occurs. Its efforts are leading to that moment. Journalism deals with the complete act of communication. If no one sees, reads, or hears the product of journalism, the learning experience is rather sterile. Of course, not all journalism courses or sequences would automatically be involved in publishing. Internships in commercial newspapers are widely used in journalism schools to provide a rowdy learning.

The 1973 College Media Advisers study found that at least 455 faculty members served as advisers to campus newspapers. Even 16 of the so-called independent-incorporated papers used journalism advisers. Eighty-five of the colleges recruited advisers from other faculty members, public relations persons, administrators, or even noncollege persons. The 13 public relations people were used primarily because they were the only persons on the campus who knew anything about putting out a newspaper.

College yearbooks were advised by journalism faculty members in 257 colleges. In 164 colleges, other faculty or administrative persons served as advisers.

In 1986, Politella believed there might be fewer advisers, but 1,268 of the 2,437 newspapers reported they had faculty advisers; 738 of 1,365 yearbooks reported faculty advisers; and 663 of 1,221 magazines reported faculty advisers. Since some of the reports sent to Politella were incomplete, the number of faculty advisers was probably higher.

The Kopenhaver-Spielberger 1989 report indicated a slightly higher number of student publications with advisers. In the 1980s, journalism faculty members were even more frequently student publications advisers because expanding journalism academic programs and courses meant more journalism faculty members were available for such assignments in more colleges.

CHAPTER 10

Administrators

Basic to the thesis found in the tales of the mythmakers is this postulate: Student publications are a vile
lot, full of obscenities and disgusting to many. College
and university trustees, presidents, and other administrators are universally arrayed as a militant force to destroy or control
such obnoxious weeds. Thus a strong and continuous battle is constantly joined between nasty student publications and administrators.
Since the power on campus is always in the hands of the administrators, who wield it in open brutal attacks or by less obvious moves, the
student press lives in constant frustration and misery.

It may be true that this dismal picture is fact on a handful of
campuses. But by and large it is totally false.

The mythmakers would be astounded to find how high is the quality of most campus student publications. Their astonishment would be
even greater to discover that college presidents and board members in
general are cordial to and supportive of freedom of the press for campus publications. Many of these people were once campus journalists.

Here are examples of college presidents who even fought for the
student press. Two are distinguished ones in which the presidents received the Alexander Meiklejohn Award of the American Association
of University Professors, the highest citation of that organization in the
field of academic freedom.

First, the story of J. W. Mauker, former president of the University
of Northern Iowa: In October 1967, a young English instructor,
Edward Hoffman, published an article in the *Northern Iowan,* the campus newspaper, criticizing the draft and the U.S. policy in Vietnam. The
position he espoused will be familiar to those who have spent even a

brief time on any American college campus in those years: American participation in the Vietnam War was profoundly immoral and should be opposed and resisted by all persons who think themselves moral agents. Specifically, the draft should be resisted as an instrument of the utter immorality of the war—by destroying draft cards, disrupting induction centers, by refusing to serve in the armed forces, and avoiding the draft. This statement, particularly its defense of mass civil disobedience toward the draft, evoked outcries of protest and demands from a variety of sources for Hoffman's ouster.

The student editor, yielding to public criticism, announced a new policy against publishing material that advocated illegal acts. President Mauker saw the need for administration leadership and support for a free student press. Perceiving the dangers of censorship in the implementation of so sweeping a prohibition, he called attention to the obligation of a university not only to refrain from suppressing but to further intellectual exchange.

> It is not enough merely to tolerate provocative ideas—the University is obligated actively to encourage the free exchange of ideas. To this end we have defined a policy for the University newspaper which provides a "free and open forum" through its letters-to-the-editor section—the only prohibitions being against libel, obscenity or extreme vulgarity. It is essential in my judgment that the forum be kept open.

Acting on this philosophy, he met with the student editor and the Board of Control of Student Publications. As a result, the policy was altered to make the standard for nonpublication not that illegal acts were advocated but that the material would "subject the editor or others responsible for the paper to civil or criminal liability." This kind of administrative involvement with student publications—to shore up student commitment to a free forum press against pressure for self-censorship from the outside —we could do with more of on American campuses.[1]

George W. Starcher, president of the University of North Dakota, also rose to the defense of the student press: Late in 1967, the student editor of the *Dakota Student* published an editorial sharply critical of the university for accepting a gift to support prizes for essays on patriotism and sportsmanship. The editorial promptly brought requests for the editor's removal. President Starcher declined to yield to the demands. "The real heart of a university," he stated subsequently, "is freedom to express and to criticize."

The incident at North Dakota occurred in the fall of 1968. Apparently a concert on the campus, supported with student funds, ended up $4,000 in the red. A student officer chose to express his sentiments by using unsold tickets to spell out in large letters on the floor the word *shit,* a term which has come, in many languages, to be used to express frustration, disappointment, and disapproval and, either in its literal or expressive meaning, can hardly be thought uncommon in the farmlands of North Dakota. In any event, it seemed a good gag, and a photograph of the ticket collage was duly printed in the student newspaper.

Apparently for many North Dakota citizens, this was only the latest confirmation of the libertinism that had set in at their university. Public demands were made, by political figures as well as private persons, for the prompt removal of the editor of the newspaper. The issue was featured in the commercial press. Newspaper editorials, columnists, and letters to the editor denounced the campus newspaper and its editor. One representative editorial called for a "fumigation of the university" and concluded by stating that the "whole incident seems to point up the crying need for college and university executives with power and the nerve to lower the boom summarily on any student, or faculty member, violating the moral standards on which this nation built its strength, honor, and greatness."

President Starcher once again resisted these pressures and in the process sought to achieve a better public understanding of the meaning and significance of academic freedom and the relationship between a university and its students. In an address to the North Dakota Farmers Union, he observed:

> Some of you have read a certain college newspaper edited by a 24-year-old youth whose success is not yet great enough to warrant the humility that accompanies greatness, and whose taste and style most people believe did, once or twice, lapse from what is becoming in the academic community, and your reaction, even though you only know what you have read or heard in the news, has been negative, even though everyone has heard, maybe even used, the word at one time or another. No one publicly condones, or even mildly approves, such exercise of freedom. Some people bearing some form of public responsibility urge firing the editor. Very few see the much more important problem of our society — I mean the unresolved questions about decency, taste, style in communication, and morals — public and private. All of our courts have sustained a standard of freedom of language that indeed makes such an incident appear like making a mountain out of a molehill. Only a few calmly ask, "Are we willing to surrender our own, and everybody's *right* to say, or print, all such words (which we shall put on a censored list) in order to get rid of one young man whose immaturity, lack of propriety, or desire to flaunt his freedom to

ignore the facts of semantics or context, irritate us? . . ."

Let me say only that America means the right of any individual to start a new religion if he feels like it, the right to participate in the free market of ideas with no facts barred, and the right to be wrong, yes, up to a certain limit and within certain bounds even the right to be offensive. Everyone of us casts his vote for a particular kind of movie when he buys a ticket, for obscenity when he buys an obscene book or magazine, and for freedom when he supports the methods of getting leadership that freedom permits.[2]

On the community college level, the president of Rockland Community College defended the right of *The Outlook,* a student publication, to freedom of the press. *The Outlook* published a poem sprinkled with obscenities. Immediately attempts were made to "set up guidelines" to control the publication. But the president opposed such efforts to censor the paper.[3]

Boards of trustees and regents regularly approve and adopt as official university policy statements developed on campus through the university's governance system. The regents of the University of Wisconsin adopted this policy, which has subsequently been the policy of all the Wisconsin colleges and universities or branches under its jurisdiction:

> The Regents of the University of Wisconsin respectfully but firmly adhere to the Board's long established policy of encouraging and supporting freedom of expression in the publication of the *Daily Cardinal* as well as in all other academic and extracurricular functions of this University. Guided by the spirit of freedom of inquiry and expression which pervades each facet of the life of this institution, the *Daily Cardinal* has earned a national reputation as a student newspaper controlled and operated by the students through their duly elected representatives. It would be destructive of the essence of the *Daily Cardinal* if any authority, whether a Regent, a Legislator, or other, could prescribe what shall be orthodox and therefore acceptable for publication and what shall be unorthodox and therefore interdicted.[4]

The Department of Journalism of Ball State University in Muncie, Indiana, has for several years been awarding citations to college administrators who have supported a free student press on the campuses. The national award is named after John R. Emens, a former Ball State president who was a staunch friend of campus student publications. Among the awards presented are the following.

In 1974, a U.S. court of appeals ruled against the University of

Mississippi for its censorship of *Bazaar,* a literary magazine that had published an issue with explicit language. Dr. Peter L. Fortune, Jr., chancellor of the University, was defendant in the suit brought by *Bazaar.* The experience was an eye-opener for Chancellor Fortune. Within a year or so, the Mississippi Board of Trustees controlling all Mississippi public colleges considered setting up a strong control system of all student publications in the state. Chancellor Fortune vigorously opposed the plan and finally prevailed to assure continued freedom for the student press. His citation said:

> This award is extended to one who stands straight and tall in support of a free student press when it would have been easier for him, personally and politically, not to do so. As Chancellor of the University of Mississippi, he dared to take a stand for a free campus press at a time when the role of a free press was not widely appreciated or approved. Singlehanded he refused to acknowledge a plan calling for firm controls on the campus press in his state. He presented another plan with the full knowledge that his own professional career could well be jeopardized. In the end, others came to see the wisdom of his plea for a free student press.

As president of the University of Texas at Arlington, Dr. Wendell H. Nedderman fought off the demands of a state legislator who felt he had been unjustly maligned by a story in the student newspaper. By refusing to meet the punitive demands of the state legislator to fire the writer, editor, faculty adviser, and publications director, he ran the considerable risk of placing his university in financial disfavor with the state legislature. In the following months, much of his time was spent mending political fences, but all the while he maintained an easy, open, and cordial relationship with the student newspaper staff and advisers.

When two student newspaper editors at Georgia Southwestern College in Americus, Georgia, were fired by their faculty adviser, they decided to take action against him in defense of their student rights to a free campus press. The man they turned to was the assistant to the academic dean, Dr. Jerry F. Williams. He immediately faced the issue by naming a new chairman of the college publications committee and later supported creation of previously nonexistent publications guidelines. These guidelines called for student editorial control of the campus newspaper and provided for new procedures to select editors and advisers. The former student editors were reinstated after adoption of the guidelines.

Dr. Jay F. Ebersole had served as dean of student services for eight years by 1981 at the Harrisburg Area Community College in Pennsylvania. During those years he consistently supported the student newspaper, *The Fourth Estate,* and defended it publicly and privately against pressures from various sources. On several occasions he took an active role in educating both the campus and the community at large regarding the nature and function of the student press. When people complained, he directed them to the editor and the student staff to wrestle with the matter. If they needed help, he provided it. When the public cried, "How can you let the students do these things?" Dean Ebersole carefully and cheerfully articulated his belief in allowing college students the freedom to learn, which includes the freedom to learn from one's mistakes.

Sometimes the complex and diverse personalities found on the campus of a university catapult the chief administrative officer from joy and pride to agony and despair. Caught in the same maelstrom are the student publications of the university. Such was the case in 1980 at Henderson State University at Arkadelphia, Arkansas, when some members of the university football team were reportedly involved in a crime. They were quickly apprehended. The editor of the *Oracle,* the campus newspaper, sought an interview with the football coach, who fumed at the editor's questions. Nonetheless, the interview was published the next day. At this point 20 members of the football team believed the coach had been unfairly treated in the story, so they collected the papers and burned them. President Martin B. Garrison issued a stern reprimand to the football players, made them pay the cost of reprinting, and commended the *Oracle.* The football players also apologized publicly.

The editors of the *DePaulia,* the student newspaper of DePaul University in Chicago found that one of the university's top administrators did not understand the role of the student press when the news was bad or gruesome. After a rape occurred on campus, the newspaper reported the cruel incident in a restrained and accurate article to alert students about such dangers. But the administrator believed the report would hurt efforts to help the coed. He had college and city police impound the paper and suspended its publication. At this point, DePaul's president, the Reverend John Richardson, interceded to reinstate the newspaper and release the hostage copies for distribution. He did even more. He arranged for a restatement of university policies to provide guidelines to prevent future restraints on the student press. DePaul University, he reports, truly believes in and welcomes a free student press on its campus.

Freedom of the press is a right guaranteed to all by the First and Fourteenth Amendments of the Constitution of the United States. Specifically, it prohibits any governmental agency or official from abridging that freedom by prior restraint, censorship, pressures, punishments, chilling actions, threats, or the power of the purse. This right has at times been misunderstood, misinterpreted, or even forgotten during the heat of battle.

Such was the case at the University of Minnesota when its board of trustees and president, despite urgent advice to the contrary by agencies of its governance system, punished the *Daily* by changing its student funding from a mandatory to a refundable fee basis. This move hindered the newspaper's operations and chilled the free expression of its student staff. The student newspaper and its editors went to court and won a resounding victory when the Eighth Circuit Court of Appeals ruled that the motivation of the university in reducing the funding was constitutionally impermissible and an obvious infringement. The university was ordered to restore the funding, to pay $30,000 of lost fee income, and to pay $153,000 in legal fees accumulated by the paper.

Standing beside the student editors in their suit was a committee on freedoms and threats from university actions. This Committee of Concerned Professors filed amicus briefs for trials in the U.S. district court and in the appeals court. Members of that committee included Professor Marcia M. Eaton, Department of Philosophy; Professor Emeritus J. Edward Gerald, School of Journalism and Mass Communication; Professor Donald M. Gillmore, School of Journalism and Mass Communication; Regents Professor Robert J. Gorlin, Department of Oral Pathology and Genetics; Professor Robert T. Holt, Department of Political Science; Regents Professor Leonard Hurwicz, Department of Economics; Professor Walter H. Johnson, Jr., Department of Physics; Professor H. E. Mason, Department of Philosophy; Professor Bernard L. Mirkin, Department of Pediatrics and Pharmacology; Professor Paul L. Murphy, Department of History; Professor V. Rama Murthy, School of Earth Sciences; Regents Professor Emeritus Alfred O. C. Nier, Department of Physics; Professor Douglas Pratt, Department of Botany; Professor Richard L. Purple, Department of Physiology and Ophthalmology; Professor Vernon W. Ruttan, Department of Agriculture Economics; Professor L. E. Scriven, Department of Chemical Engineering and Materials Science; Regents Professor John E. Turner, Department of Political Science; and Professor Finn Wold, Department of Biochemistry.

In 1968, the Louisiana Tech University campus newspaper, *The Tech Talk,* became a student newspaper. The change from a faculty organ to a true student newspaper came about at the insistence of the president of the university, Dr. F. Jay Taylor. The new student newspaper almost immediately rocked the university and community with their first taste of student opinion, including criticism of the university administration, calls to pull down the Confederate flags that flew on campus, and the hiring of the newspaper's first black student journalist.

This new and heady atmosphere of free expression and openness resulted in all of the predictable difficulties for the university in general and the president in particular. Despite threatening calls, garbage thrown onto his lawn, and criticism from political powers and others accustomed to a "safe" campus newspaper, Dr. Taylor remained steadfast in his unconditional support of a free student press. This support has continued for every year thereafter.

In 1987 the president of Western Kentucky University commanded national headlines when he directed a subcommittee on publications to consider establishing faculty editors for the school newspaper and yearbook. He also advocated giving a publication committee some editorial control over the publications.

Objections to this plan were immediate and massive. When the president resigned at the end of the Spring 1988 term, Thomas Meredith, as the new president, walked into the maelstrom with the issue still unsettled. With decisiveness and without ambiguity, he declared his belief that student publications should be run by students. There should be no editorial control by administrators or faculty.

For his strong endorsement of freedom of the student press in 1990, Meredith was awarded the 1991 Emens citation.

CHAPTER 11

Guidelines
and Policies

As a result of campus disruptions several years ago, many colleges and universities have adopted statements or policies generally called a students' bill of rights. These statements emphasize due process in handling student problems. Almost all of them contain assurance of a free campus press.

The genesis of these bills of rights came primarily from recommendations made by a committee of the American Association of University Professors (AAUP). Although some colleges have rewritten the AAUP ideas into a tyrannical plan of control, hundreds of other colleges, public and private alike, now follow as university policy the endorsement of a free press on campus.

Here is a typical statement, adopted by Wichita State University in 1968 and followed for several years:

> The student press and radio shall be free of censorship and advance approval of copy.
>
> Editors and managers of student communications shall be protected from arbitrary suspension and removal because of student, faculty, administrative, or public disapproval of editorial policy or content. Only for proper and stated causes shall editors and managers be subject to removal. The agency responsible for the appointment of editors and managers shall be the agency responsible for their removal, such action subject to the Dean of Students' ratification and, on appeal, decision of the Student-Faculty Court.
>
> All University published and financed student communications shall explicitly state on the editorial page or in broadcast that the opinions that are expressed by them are not necessarily those of the college, university, or student body.[1]

For the expression of contrary views, equal time and space should be allowed for those wishing to express their views.[2] A student, group, or organization may publish and distribute written material on campus without prior approval of the content of the material but the time, place, and manner of distribution may be limited by such reasonable written regulations as are necessary for the operation of the university.

The student press shall be free of censorship. The editors and managers shall not be arbitrarily suspended because of student, faculty, administration, alumni, or community disapproval of editorial policy or content. Similar freedom is assured oral statements of views on university-controlled and student-run radio or television stations. This editorial freedom entails a corollary obligation under the canons of responsible journalism and applicable regulations of the Federal Communications Commission.

Freedom of expression is of even greater importance to the academic community than it is to the society at large. "The right to know" and "the right to criticize," cornerstones of a free press in a free society, are also foundation stones of a free academy. The printed word may properly be thought of as the lifeblood of learning, and faculty and student publications will therefore occupy a central place in the academic community. The student press can help to establish and maintain an atmosphere of free and responsible discussion and intellectual exploration on the campus. It can be a means of bringing student concerns to the attention of the faculty and the institutional authorities and of formulating student opinion on various issues on the campus and in the world at large. To those ends, the Publications Board is constituted by the President, acting on behalf of the academic community, to serve as publisher of student publications and to exercise the powers and responsibilities of the publisher on behalf of the institution.[4]

The student press should be free of censorship and advance approval of copy, and its editors and managers should be free to develop their own editorial policies and news coverage.

Editors and managers should subscribe to canons of responsible journalism. At the same time, they should be protected from arbitrary suspension and removal because of student, faculty, administrative, or public disapproval of editorial policy or content. Only for proper and stated causes should editors and managers be subject to removal and then by orderly and prescribed procedures.

There is established the Student Publications Policy Committee ("Student" modifies "Publications"). The Student Publications Policy Committee is a standing committee of the Student Affairs Council. It acts in all matters pertaining to those publications written primarily by students and financed by University-sanctioned student fees. It has no jurisdiction over official University, administrative, or departmental publications no matter how authored.[5]

Truthfully, the student press on most campuses enjoys considerable understanding, support, and freedom. Universities should encourage the development of guidelines and general policies for student publications on this basis.

1. The guidelines should be fairly short.
2. The guidelines should not be argumentative.
3. The guidelines should clearly meet every constitutional test concerning freedom of the press and due process.
4. Language should be precise and avoid generalizations.
5. By all means, abstract terms should not appear in the guidelines.

An *abstraction* is a term that allows for any person to apply it as an inspiring umbrella over selected facts or philosophical orientations.

Here are some practical and constitutionally acceptable guidelines and policy approaches.

1. The First Amendment and the Fourteenth Amendment to the U.S. Constitution protect the rights of students to free speech and free press.

2. Student publications (newspapers, yearbooks, magazines, etc.) and electronic facilities (radio, television, film, video or sound tapes, closed circuit, cable, or wired wireless) serve as educational tools, as means of expression for students and the public, as forums for discourse on issues, and as sources of entertainment and enlightenment.

3. Students have the right to report and editorialize on events, ideas, and issues in the school, community, nation, and world, even though these may be unpopular or controversial.

4. Students should be encouraged but not required to seek and present contrasting views.

5. Students should have the legal and ethical practices expected of professional journalists called to their attention.

6. Students should know about applicable laws pertaining to libel, slander, obscenity, privacy, copyright, and substantial disruption of school activities, and should consider accepted community standards of decency and good taste. The laws are quite technical and should also be understood by school officials.

7. Students should consult with and consider the views of their print and broadcast advisers regarding the content of their student publications or broadcast programs.

8. Students have the right to determine the content of student publications and broadcast programs. The student editor in chief or student station manager is the person exercising free press rights and making all final decisions concerning content of the publications or broadcast programs, including advertisements.

9. School officials should seek qualified advisers and should support the print and electronic programs with adequate budgets.

10. Advisers and students should be encouraged to seek the counsel of professional print and broadcast journalists, who should be willing to provide such advice.

11. Journalism advisers should be assisted and supported by administrators and trustee boards in implementing guidelines.

12. Boards of trustees and administrators should inform students, faculty, and the public of the guidelines.

13. Student publications may provide salaries, wages, commissions, grants-in-aid, or scholarships to designated student staff members.

14. Editors and managers of student publications cannot be dismissed because of student, faculty, staff, administrative, or public disapproval of editorial policy or content.

15. Student staff members, in consultation with their faculty advisers, may expend funds through appropriate channels from their designated budgets.

16. Any merchandise or service that may legally be sold to or used by students may be advertised in student publications.

17. Each student publication should have a faculty adviser.

18. Faculty advisers advise students, but do not assume financial deficits or losses incurred by student publications.

19. Student staff members are solely responsible for all editorial content of the student publications. Student publications must be free of censorship and advance approval of copy. Editors and managers are free to develop their own editorial and news coverage or content. Freedom of the press as guaranteed by the Constitution of the United States and by state constitutions is not impeded or interfered with by this university or any of its agencies, staff, faculty, or administrators.

Item 19 should be established by action of the board of trustees of a state university. Private colleges should also establish this policy by board action, as many have. Any articles of incorporation involved should also specify these policies and practices.

Student journalists, publication advisers, and college officials should be vigilant in efforts to understand and protect free press rights on the campus. There are several danger signals that should alert these leaders about developing problems, especially when they appear on public college campuses. The policies and practices in the preceding guidelines would forestall serious problems causing campus disruptions. Here is a listing of danger signals.

1. The college emphasizes that its student publications program is designed to create a favorable image with its constituencies.

2. Because of higher priorities, funding provided for student publications must be reduced or even eliminated.

3. "The college is really a family, and all are expected to be good family members."

4. A student publication is a student club subject to club regulations.

5. A student publication is under the jurisdiction of the student government and is answerable to it.

6. A student publication is under the jurisdiction of the student personnel department and is answerable to it.

7. A student publication is under the jurisdiction of a publications board and is answerable to it.

8. A student publication is under the jurisdiction of a public relations officer and is answerable for its impact on public relations.

9. A student publication must or may be subject to a hearing board to answer and adjust complaints.

10. A student publication must comply with directives of the college business division regarding editorial and advertising content.

11. A student publication must negotiate its financial allocations on a subjective basis controlled by the state agencies.

12. A student publication is directed by journalism faculty members (who in effect serve as the editors).

13. A college official is designated as publisher, with ill-defined authority.

14. College officials make statements urging or demanding that student journalists write and publish responsibly, but they do not explain what that means.

15. Journalism faculty members refuse to serve as advisers to the student publication. The college refuses to allocate duty time for such advising.

16. A special committee of administrators, faculty, and students is appointed to restructure the operations and role of the student publica-

tion. Few, if any, of the student publication staff members are on this committee. Such committees frequently are assigned the duty to weaken the publication.

17. Recommendations are made that the student publication become incorporated and be removed from the campus.

18. Regulations concerning content of advertising and editorial matters are imposed or suggested.

19. Requiring approval of any kind prior to publication.

20. Maintaining a system of punishments for material published.

21. Requiring that potentially libelous material, material that may invade privacy, or material that may be pornographic not be published.

22. Requiring that student staff members must have taken certain courses or maintain a certain grade point average or carry a minimum course load.

23. Failure of the board of trustees to stipulate that no agent of the college may infringe upon the press freedom of students.

24. Student staff members are required to adhere to the code of ethics of a professional group or an administrative committee.

25. A new college president or other new top administrators bring with them what they call or what appears to be a determination to straighten out a weak institution.

26. Maintenance of a student-operated court or judicial system authorized to punish fellow students, including student journalists.

27. Direct pressure or public statements attacking student publications staff members for content are used as threats to the exercise of free press rights.

28. Editors or staff members are fired, or even dismissed from college, by administrative agencies for content of the publication.

It must be emphasized that these danger signals should be of concern and serve as warnings to college administrators who do not want to restrict campus press freedom. Vagueness and lack of clarity are enemies alike of press freedom and good college administration.

CHAPTER 12

Private Colleges

Most of the materials presented in this book focus on student publications in public colleges. Material is also available about private colleges. Bob Hendrickson, an adviser at the School of the Ozarks in Point Lookout, Missouri, presented a report on the variables in organizations and press freedom in private colleges and universities for the 1987 national autumn convention of College Media Advisers.[1]

His report, with added commentary in brackets, follows.

Realistic, professional, thorough ought to be the adjectives which describe the journalism programs in any college or university, but that is not always an accurate description. The great variety and diversity of institutions of higher education is an asset in the United States, but there is not space or facility nor appropriateness for an equal amount of diversity within the professional standards of most academic disciplines or within the limits of the interpretation or even the spirit of the laws of free press. At the time of this writing, state colleges and universities know exactly where they stand regarding free press because they are protected by the First and Fourteenth Amendments of the Constitution; however, that is not the case in private colleges and universities since administrative officers in private institutions do not function as state officials.

[The courts have been tussling with the problem of the public functional nature of private colleges who receive federal funds, as do many of their students. The private college, moreover, performs a public or "state" function in the way it operates and serves its constituencies. One court has held that a private university could not add restrictions to its already established public-forum provision; in another case a private college lost its legal right to sue for libel because it had thrust itself into the public-figure category.

Andres Ciofalo, associate professor of media studies at Loyola College in Baltimore, proposed that students in private colleges attempt as a legal cloak the First Amendment concept of academic freedom to base a constitutional right upon. Ciofalo's article in the 1987–1988 fall and winter issue of *College Media Review*[2] said the academic freedom shield could also attract critical appraisals from accrediting agencies, honor societies, and other educational organizations.]

One of the assets of private institutions of higher education is the diversity they provide in purposes, ideals, and objectives, but in that diversity, there are significant differences in the organizations and functions of journalism programs and the publication of college newspapers. The nature of that diversity is important because of the important role that the press plays in our society and the responsibility it has for ensuring an informed public through the dissemination of information. Some concern should be given to the status of free press in private colleges because if it is not there, a successful journalism program is unlikely. Before any vague assumptions or generalizations are made about the status of a free press in private educational institutions, consideration should be given to assessments based on information which discerns the status or presence of free press, various organizational structures of journalism programs, and the distribution of authority for publications in private colleges and universities. Consequently, the following presents the results of a survey of journalism programs in private colleges and universities. The responses to survey questions are given in percentages, and the responses are followed by a few observations and recommendations.

For the study, the *Cass College Newspaper Sourcebook,* 1986–87, published by Cass Communications, Inc., was used as the source of a list of colleges and universities in the United States. *Cass* identifies among all the colleges and universities listed 386 private colleges and universities. A random sample of sixty was chosen by selecting every sixth private college or private university. This procedure yielded a total of sixty institutions which were mailed a questionnaire. These were mailed to a faculty adviser for the college newspaper. A second random sample of sixty colleges was selected and questionnaires mailed to student editors of college and university newspapers. Approximately 60 percent of the questionnaires were returned, thus ensuring a statistically valid random sample. The number count of the responses to the questions has been converted to percentages rounded to the nearest whole number. The questionnaire had 26 questions in a random sequence. Related questions were not presented in a sequence of any logical order. For the purposes of reporting the information, the questions and answers have been reorganized under five topics: (1) organizational structure and decision making; (2) management; (3) academic relationships; (4) professional affiliations; and (5) free press.

The results of the questionnaire are as follows:

Organizational Structure

Six of the questions pertain to organizational structure and decision making routings of college and university newspapers. The responses to these inquiries are relevant to free press questions for a number of reasons.

Faculty advisers report that student editors have a final decision for determining newspaper content for 63 percent of the papers. For 13 percent of the remaining papers, the faculty adviser has the final say; the president has the final say for 10 percent of the papers; the publication boards and deans or students each have the last word for 6 percent each.

Student editors' responses revealed no significant differences:

- —70 percent: student editors have the final word
- —13 percent: faculty advisers
- —3 percent: college presidents

The question pertinent to these percentages is, "If the adviser or president reads the paper prior to publication in order to say what can go in the paper and what cannot, is that not censorship by prior restraint, and is that not contrary to the spirit of the law? It would most likely be a case of prior restraint in a state school." If the intent is to advise, educate, or assist in the improvement of the paper, that should be expected in an educational institution, but to organize the publication of the news so that it is routinely censored is no way to train journalists [or for that matter to produce a timely newspaper. The clumsiness of arranging to have the president examine each issue prior to publication would impose impossible duties upon the president].

Reporting on who is the designated publisher, advisers report the following:

- —For 23 percent of the papers, the college is the publisher.
- —For 23 percent of the papers, the student government is the publisher.
- —In 6 percent of the colleges, the president is the publisher.
- —In 6 percent, faculty advisers are the publishers.

Similarly, student editors report that in 26 percent of their schools, the college is designated the publisher; 36 percent of the colleges have identified the student government as the publisher; and in 13 percent of the colleges, the adviser is also the publisher.

Personally, many advisers would not want to serve as both adviser and publisher, but others might be so inclined.

[The confusion about what the word *publisher* really means is demonstrated by these responses. If the publisher is a person who has the traditional function of controlling the content of a publication, then it seems doubtful that the president, the student government, or even the adviser really does this. In some cases, yes; in many cases, no. Being owner of the publication and accepting financial responsibility for its operations still creates a definitional problem.] There is not a significant difference in these figures, but the general impression is that the majority of newspaper advisers are not educated in journalism.

There is another question, however, that is related to the status of faculty advisers in private colleges and universities which gives us the following information:

From newspaper advisers:

1. 60 percent of them are not journalism teachers.
2. 36 percent of them are journalism teachers.

From student editors:

1. 33 percent do not have advisers.
2. 9 percent have advisers who are journalism teachers.
3. 58 percent of the advisers are not journalism teachers.

[It seems appropriate that colleges should provide at least some journalism courses and employ advisers qualified in journalism. Financial, curricular, or enrollment limitations affect this ability. Even with no adviser or poorly trained advisers and with no journalism courses, students in private colleges manage to produce student publications.]

There is no significant difference in the procedures used for selecting student editors as reported by faculty advisers and student editors. In 34 percent of the institutions, editors are selected by a publication board; 57 percent of the editors are selected by the current and outgoing newspaper staff; 6 percent of the editors are selected by the administration.

Management

Faculty advisers report that in 36 percent of the colleges, newspaper budgets are managed by student government, and 23 percent of the advisers said at one time or another, student government has withheld funds.

[Student government finds itself in a quandary with the student publications it sponsors or finances. It, like other government agencies, frequently decides the student press must support all government ideas and actions. But the student press, as part of its responsibility to student readers, will from time to time become sharply critical of student government actions or officials. Student government persons believe too often that they should discipline those student journalists. An easy way to attempt to do that is to reduce or eliminate funding or the publication. This tactic is an unacceptable situation in the United States, in public or private colleges, where we find commitment to First Amendment values to be paramount in our philosophy. Student publications funding should not depend upon the vagaries of campus student politics or ambitions.]

According to faculty advisers, 73 percent of the newspapers in their colleges are financed by student fees and advertisements. Student editors report that only 40 percent of their papers are supported by student fees and ads, and 33 percent of their papers are supported by colleges' budgets, which is a significant difference from faculty adviser reports. Only 20 percent of the papers are supported as college or university budgeted expense.

[Complete financial records and reports of all publications income and expenditures should be maintained at all times so student staff members can experience the management realities of the publication world. Fund allocations should not be used to obtain favorable content.]

Academic Relationships

Faculty advisers and student editors present about the same statistics describing relationships between academic programs in journalism and the college newspapers, but there are differences reported in how academic programs relate to newspaper publication.

In 65 to 70 percent of the colleges, the newspaper is not part of the academic program. Advisers report that 83 percent of the newspapers operate independently of classes and are an extracurricular activity. According to student editors, 76 percent of the papers are operated independently from journalism classes. According to advisers and editors approximately 25 percent of the students involved in newspaper publication receive academic credit, and about the same percentages of colleges and universities offer a major in journalism.

The most significant difference in the responses from advisers and student editors regarding the academic programs and their relationship to newspapers pertains to reviewing the paper. Advisers report that a publication board meets periodically to review the paper in 43 percent of the colleges; student editors report that this happens in 23 percent of the colleges. Advisers report that in 40 percent of their colleges, journalism classes review the paper; student editors report that that sort of review or evaluation happens in 10 percent of their colleges.

These statistics are likely to attract attention from the majority of advisers and student editors, because their papers are fairly independent operations; these statistics may cause concern among those who use the newspaper as an extension of the journalism program. Those two alternatives represent the operational structures of college newspapers—they are either independent operations or they have close operational ties to journalism classes. The majority are independent.

Professional Affiliations

Faculty advisers and student editors report that approximately 68 percent of the colleges do not offer membership or have affiliation with a professional journalism society. They report that only about 30 percent of the faculty advisers are members of a professional journalism society.

[Student publications should provide invaluable learning experiences for journalism and other students. This can and does occur in a variety of ways, ranging from informal friendliness to structured formal laboratory or class projects. None of these necessarily interfere with students' press freedom. Association with professional journalists, in their organizations or in other ways, would be of great benefit to advisers, journalism teachers, and students.]

Free Press

Sixty-six percent of the advisers of college newspapers say that their paper adheres to First Amendment rights for free press; 13 percent say their paper does not; 6 percent do not know. The response of student editors is almost exactly the same.

Only 5 percent of college papers are read by public relations officers or other information officers prior to printing. Faculty advisers report that 10 percent of the papers are censored by administrators. Student editors report 3 percent.

According to the faculty advisers, only 40 percent have published guidelines or a publication handbook. Student editors report that 63 percent of them have published guidelines to follow. That is a significant difference.

When asked if their college newspapers adhere to a published code of ethics, 60 percent of the faculty advisers say yes, 33 percent say no, and 12 percent do not know. Student editors respond with a significant difference—40 percent yes, 46 percent no.

Faculty advisers report that 26 percent of their colleges have written statements which insure free press, 66 percent say they do not, and 8 percent do not know. Student editors report no significant difference except 20 percent of them do not know if the college has a written policy which insures free press.

[Obviously, there is confusion about the level of press freedom accorded student journalists, the existence of publications policies, and the commitment to ethical journalism. Many of the difficulties that occur could be ameliorated by written policies and provisions that could explain the operations of the student publications and provide protection for free expression on the part of student journalists.]

Observation and Recommendations

Since approximately 80 percent of the newspapers in private colleges and universities function independently of the academic program and are regarded as extra-curricular, and since approximately 60 percent of the advisers are not journalism teachers, and since 33 percent of the newspapers have no adviser, it is surprising that other statistics are not worse than they are. Only 10 percent of the papers are censored by the administration.

A second observation is that 68 percent of the newspapers have no affiliations with professional journalism organizations, and the fact that they do not probably has some significance to the statistics that report that 34 percent of the papers do not adhere to First Amendment rights or do not know if they do or not. Only 30 percent of the advisers are affiliated with a journalism society and 33 percent of the papers surveyed have no adviser. These statistics can lead to the assumption that some of those responsible for newspaper production in private colleges and universities are not as well informed as they should be for their own protection.

A third observation is that an important question was not asked of student editors. Knowing whether or not editors intended to pursue journalism as a career would have been valuable for making recommendations. If editors intend to pursue a career in journalism, a number of recommendations could be made about the benefits of journalism societies, the prudence of knowing about law and ethics of journalism, etc.

A fourth observation is that according to advisers, 26 percent of their colleges have a written statement that attempts to ensure free press, 66 percent do not, and 8 percent do not know. The statistics for student editors is about the same except 20 percent do not know if such a statement exists or not.

Recommendation

Since private colleges and universities are not ensured free press rights by the First and Fourteenth Amendments as fully as state institutions are, it is herein recommended that private institutions formulate policy statements that provide for a free student press. The assumption is that policy statements approved by the administration and included in official literature become binding by common contract law. There is sufficient court precedent to give credence to this procedure. The fact is that the courts have not decided that the First and Fourteenth Amendments do not apply to private institutions, but in the meantime, common contract law may provide college newspapers press freedom. If it does not do so in fact, it is a sufficient base for establishing written policies and guidelines which at present do not exist in the majority of private colleges. Establishing written policies is beneficial for everyone concerned. Such documents protect everyone involved in the production of newspapers by defining roles, responsibilities, and procedures. In a private college, when no documentation exists, all decision making is the administration's prerogative.

[When college administrators make decisions, they can easily become embroiled in campus unrest when those decisions are not legally supportable under any of a number of statutes. So far, so few cases involving press freedom in private colleges have been brought to court that no one really knows what the courts would decide in specific litigation.]

The development of written policy and procedures provides a basis for smooth operation during routine times, and sanity and rational responses when trouble comes. Anyone who has worked with college newspapers will not need examples of irate or irrational responses from readers, students, faculty, or administrators.

A final recommendation in response to the results of the survey reported is that the Committee for Private Colleges and Universities of College Media Advisers consider the diversity in the state of free press in private schools and formulate some means or procedure to raise the conscious need for private schools to work toward a more consistent insistence on free press in all colleges and universities.

Theories for Freedom of the Press

The First Amendment became effective as constitutional law on December 15, 1791, when Virginia ratified the Bill of Rights, fifteen years after the Declaration of Independence had been proclaimed.

The First Amendment provides that Congress shall make no law respecting

1. an establishment of religion (freedom from state religion);
2. or prohibiting the free exercise thereof (freedom of religion);
3. or abridging the freedom of speech (freedom of speech);
4. or of the press (freedom of the press);
5. or the right of the people peaceably to assemble (freedom of assembly);
6. or to petition the government for a redress of grievances (freedom to petition).

In 1798 Congress ignored the First Amendment to provide the Alien and Sedition Acts to eliminate criticism of the government. But the laws were so unpopular that they were not reenacted when Thomas Jefferson became president. This also marked the end of any federal libel laws. The Supreme Court ruled in the nineteenth century that the First Amendment pertained only to federal government officials and agencies.

In 1868, the United States added the Fourteenth Amendment to the Constitution. It was inspired in the Reconstruction days following the Civil War partly to protect former slaves. The Supreme Court from 1873 until 1925 believed it pertained primarily to property rights and did not cover the civil rights described in the Bill of Rights. But the landmark 1925 *Gitlow* decision saw the Court reverse this view and rule that the Fourteenth Amendment umbrella did include all constitutional rights. The decision and the Fourteenth Amendment provide that

1. The First Amendment restraint on Congress was extended to all branches and all levels of government and to all government officials.

2. Rights guaranteed in the Constitution cannot be taken away from persons by governmental agencies unless due process is carefully followed.

3. Constitutional, federal, state, municipal, and common law and all governmental regulations must apply to and protect equally all persons.

The Supreme Court and other courts believe that provisions in the Constitution can be set aside if the state (the government) can present evidence that it has a serious and compelling interest to prevent a danger greater than the loss of a right. During the nineteenth century, courts believed they could set aside free speech or free press rights if published material would have an evil tendency.

This early test was whether the expression had the tendency to pose a threat of an evil that would damage the morality or character of a person most unable to cope with such material. This was later modified by considering whether there was a reasonable tendency. In the early 1900s the Supreme Court developed the stronger requirement that the material had to pose a clear and present or a substantial threat of danger.

In 1925, the Supreme Court in its landmark *Gitlow* decision ruled that the Fourteenth Amendment did cover and include all the rights in the First Amendment. Thus freedom of the press became guaranteed to all persons and was protected from all levels of government and all government officials, federal, state, or local.

A view that the First Amendment specified the six principal rights because of its position and their importance guided the thinking of many judges who believed freedom of speech and freedom of the press thus held a preferred position superior to other rights.

But the Supreme Court was confronted with difficult decisions when cases presented conflicts between the many rights provided by the body of the Constitution and its amendments. To arrive at decisions, the Court began balancing rights against each other on the basis of the specific litigatory factors involved for a twentieth-century test.

The commitment to robust and lively debate established the "public forum" test, which indicates that once a forum actively has been established, the government cannot weaken or discontinue it because of its content. The courts have long respected the concept of a marketplace of ideas wherein viewpoints contend for acceptance. "Forum" does not mean that the press medium must provide space for various viewpoints. Presenting only one view may be proper under the First Amendment.

Following World War II, under the impetus of an informal commission that proposed that the press should operate in a socially responsible manner, there has appeared a belief that the institutional press should be required through some mechanism to provide access to all persons wanting space to express viewpoints. This access concept has been strongly resisted by the press and has been consistently ruled against by the courts. Some courts, however, ask the press to be both free and responsible in function and performance and to have the promotion of the public welfare as an objective. Other courts and many persons consider this philosophical orientation to pose dangerous threats to freedom of the press.

At one end of the spectrum of the tests is the belief that freedom of speech and of the press are absolutes and should be totally unregulated for content at all times and in all situations. Additional views the courts have utilized include

- A belief that if the state has a sufficiently compelling reason to protect a valid state interest, the First Amendment may be set aside.
- Material can be regulated or denied to children who have not reached maturity levels sufficient to cope with such materials.
- It is desirable to measure First Amendment values in terms of the intended meaning the original framers of the United States Constitution and the Bill of Rights had in mind.
- In contemporary society institutional or corporate rights are probably more significant than individual rights.

All of these theories pose problems to First Amendment provisions, so the late twentieth century is still debating rights.

Freedom of the press cannot be infringed by an agency of the state unless that agency can demonstrate a compelling state need or interest to impose such restraint. Even so, the state agency must provide specific rules and regulations that are not vague, overbroad, or overpunitive, must provide adequate due process procedures and appeals pertaining to those restraints, and bears the burden of proof in justifying any such restraints.

Courts have ruled that First Amendment protection may or may not cover the following areas, depending upon the specific circumstances.

• Actions and conduct alone are not protected; however, if they contain an element of expressiveness, even symbolically, they may be entitled to at least some First Amendment protection.

• "Fighting words," which invite lawless reactions, are not protected if they are personally abusive epithets which when addressed to the ordinary citizen are, as a matter of common knowledge, likely to provoke violent actions. However, expressions that stir people to anger, invite public argument, cause unrest, or create merely an apprehension of disturbance are not fighting words.

• Substantial threats to national security are not protected, but the threat must be real, not simply severe critical appraisal or revelation of embarrassing but constitutionally protected information.

• Obscenity, if it fails the provisions specified by the Supreme Court in its 1973 *Miller* decision, is not protected. In effect, constitutionally unprotected obscenity pertains primarily to hard-core pornography or scatological depictions. The Supreme Court has, however, ruled that depictions of children engaging in sexual activities are so odious that they have no constitutional protection.

• Defamation, which can be either libel or slander, is not protected by the First Amendment unless legal justification for its publication or voicing can be presented under provisions of state law. There is also a federal defense available under provisions of the *New York Times* decision of 1964 concerning public officials and public figures.

The First Amendment does not protect journalists in their newsgathering activities, in forcing government or private agencies to provide access to information, from not having to reveal the confidentiality of news sources, or in a right not to respond to subpoenas or not to honor search warrants. A number of state and federal statutes provide such protection, which has proven to be very effective in many instances but not of great value in others.

Commercial product advertising is not protected by the First Amendment in that it can be regulated reasonably by state or federal agencies and laws. However, advertising that presents ideas, information, political advocacy, editorial views, or opinions does enjoy First Amendment protection.[1]

There are differing views of just what is the best legal theory or argument to present to a court in proceedings involving student publications. Dr. John David Reed, chair of the Department of Journalism at Eastern Illinois University and of the Press Law Committee of College Media Advisers, conducted a doctoral study titled "Toward a Theory of the First Amendment for the College Press."[2] He concluded that the strongest response to First Amendment restraint and litigation could be the editorial discretion of the student editor. He wrote:

> Sandwiched between the Supreme Court's early landmark interpretations of the press clause in *Near v. Minnesota* and *Grosjean v. American Press Co.* was the case of the Reveille Seven, student editors and supporters of the Louisiana State University newspaper who were expelled after objecting to the school's censorship of a letter critical of the state's governor, Huey Long. The case received national attention, including a scholarship offer to the students to finish their last semester at the School of Journalism at the University of Missouri at Columbia. At the fiftieth reunion of their 1935 graduation, a span which included a host of Supreme Court decisions reaffirming the principles of *Near* and lower court rulings extending the reach of the First Amendment to the college press, one of the seven told an audience, "We were dismissed for practicing the ideals we were being taught. The same thing could happen to you. Things haven't changed that much."[3]

The conclusion of that comment, its warning, and its premise provide a framework for addressing the questions about the college press, newspapers, and other publications produced principally by students as extracurricular activities and serving primarily student readerships on college and university campuses, and the First Amendment: How has the college press fared in the courts? Have the courts distinguished it from the commercial press? Have the principles established by those courts adequately protected it from the government interference forbidden by the First Amendment?

Its conclusion, that the state through its university government still can with impunity punish or restrain the college press, is not the lesson of the body of law resulting from the college press cases. Things have changed, at least on public college campuses such as Louisiana State University: In all but two of the fifty-one reported decisions, the First Amendment has stood as a barrier against government abridgement of freedom of the college press. The answer to the first question, then, is that judicial application of the First Amendment to the college press, in its results, has responded adequately to the commands of the First Amendment.

The accuracy of the Reveille Seven warning, however, was well taught by the holdings or in the dicta of some of the college press cases: The expulsion of the editor of the Colorado School of Mines *Oredigger* for using offensive language in his newspaper was upheld,[4] and the editors of the *Royal Purple* at the University of Wisconsin at Whitewater were compelled to publish material they had rejected;[5] the propriety of firing the editor of the Troy State University *Tropolitan* for criticizing state government was implied;[6] and the possibility that the editor of the North Carolina Central University *Campus Echo* could be compelled to publish material he chose not to publish was suggested.[7] At the same time, a majority of the courts in balancing the interests in conflict in the college press decisions have relied on precisely the standards and underlying values described by the Supreme Court in its interpretation of the press clause of the First Amendment.

The answer to another question, then, is mixed. First, in thirty-three cases where controls were attempted by non-campus agencies, the courts — including the Supreme Court in *Zurcher v. Stanford Daily* — have applied to the college press the principles established in traditional interpretation of commercial press cases: Where prior restraints were involved, the press has been placed in a preferred position on a scale weighted by heavy burdens against infringement; where subsequent punishment was threatened, a rigid clear and present danger test was imposed; and only where news gathering and individual torts were involved were press rights balanced evenly against other interests. Similarly, neither have the courts distinguished the college press under the First Amendment in eleven of the twenty-nine cases involving control by or through campus administrations: The same exacting standards were employed against attempted censorship and the chilling effects of punishment. But in fifteen other decisions in the latter group, courts have drawn or suggested distinctions in defining the principles for application of the First Amendment to the college press, eschewing rigorous application of those preferred tests arising from press clause interpretation and focusing instead on a balancing of interests under diluted tests of interference both prior and subsequent to publication.

The inconsistency of the courts in applying First Amendment principles to the unique characteristics of the college press — the disciplinary and proprietary relationships between it and the university it serves — has sent confusing signals. Some college administrators continue to fire editors, and some courts continue to view college newspapers as First Amendment poor sisters: Shortly before the Reveille Seven recounted how they were fired for practicing the ideals taught by *Near,* for instance, the editor of the Humboldt State University *Lumberjack* was fired for endorsing political candidates,[8] and the editors at the Portland Community College *Bridge* were compelled by a federal judge to publish material they had rejected.[9] The preliminary answer to the question, then, is that the principles arising from the college press cases have not been adequate, at least in the practical sense.

Whether or not those principles are constitutionally adequate depends upon the validity of the hypothesis of this study: That distinguishing the Constitutional protection of the college press because it is "owned otherwise" — that is, because of either the proprietary or disciplinary relationship between it and the government of the community which it serves — abridges the press clause freedoms of the college press and therefore runs afoul of the Constitutional guarantee of the First Amendment. Although the following analysis applies only to the college press at state-supported institutions, it also holds implications for the private campus. The courts have developed two approaches in applying the First Amendment to the college press, identified in this study as the concepts of editorial discretion — which focuses on protection of the editorial decision-making process through the press clause — and the public forum, which focuses on assuring access for expressive activity to facilities used by the public primarily through the speech and association clauses. Those decisions which have drawn no distinctions between the college and commercial press have relied on the former concept; where such distinctions have been drawn or suggested, the latter concept has been applied. It is against the public forum approach, then, that the validity of the hypothesis must be tested.

Public Forum Approach: Unconstitutional Distinctions

In the fifteen college press cases the courts have relied on the public forum approach to distinguish the college press under the First Amendment, or to suggest that they could, the competing interest has been either the university's need to protect the campus environment or its proprietary relationship to its publications. Under the former rationale, the courts have reduced both the scope and the standards for protection of the college press, holding or suggesting that schools could control content which was offensive,[10] embarrassing,[11] or "short of legal obscenity,"[12] and imposing such watered-down barriers as *"apt to be* significantly disruptive"[13] against subsequent punishment.[14] Under the latter rationale, the courts have held or suggested that the school can limit both users and uses of a student publication,[15] can control content for purposes of protecting against libel,[16] can compel publication to protect its reputation[17] or to assure access to a publication's columns,[18] and can punish publication of criticism.[19]

Development of the public forum approach in the courts and in the literature addressing the question has been in response to the university's proprietary relationship to the college press. That the college press could be distinguished under the public forum approach was apparent in the first college press case, *Dickey v. Alabama State Board of Education,* which overturned the expulsion but implied approval of the firing of a student editor for his criticism of the paper's ultimate owners,[20] and has been developed in such cases as *Antonelli v. Hammond,* which held that the school was *"not necessarily* the unrestrained master of what it creates and fosters,"[21] and *Bazaar v. Fortune,* which explored the public forum rationale in detail.[22] The concept has been reiterated and expanded upon in most of the literature, as noted earlier.[23]

In accepting the distinctions resulting from application of the public forum approach, those analysts, as well as the courts, have based their conclusions on certain presumptions about the environment and nature of the college press, about the Supreme Court's development of the public forum doctrine, and about the functions and priorities as well as the standards and values of various expression clauses of the First Amendment. Whether or not the abridgments of the college press authorized by the public forum approach imperil achievement of the values underlying the Court's interpretation of the press clause depends upon the constitutional soundness of those presumptions.

In identifying the appropriate standards for assessing interference with college press rights, the public forum approach relies on two presumptions about the environment and nature of the college press. The first is that there are no significant distinctions between high school and college levels: one recent study asserts that "the theory underlying the holdings in [college press cases] should be applicable to the high school setting."[24] The second is implicit in the failure of the approach to recognize the distinctions in application of standards to press and other forms of expression protected by the First Amendment. Neither proposition is constitutionally sound.

The former disregards the emphasis of several college press courts on the factor of maturity of college-age students,[25] as well as the distinctions drawn by the Supreme Court: in *Tinker v. Des Moines Independent School District,* for example, the Court established a diluted version of the clear and present danger test as a barrier to prior restraint at the high school level,[26] but in *Papish v. Board of Curators of the University of Missouri* the Court insisted that at the college level, "the First Amendment leaves no room for the operation of a dual standard."[27] The latter presumption fails to acknowledge that the Supreme Court has required more stringent standards of protection in its press clause interpretation, where press expression often stands in a preferred position, than in its application of public forum theory, which balances expression against the state's interest in regulating time, place, and manner of distribution facilities established for other uses: in *New York Times v. United States,* for instance, the Court imposed a heavy burden on prior restraint,[28] but in *Southeastern Promotions, Ltd. v. Conrad* the Court noted after reviewing its application of the public forum doctrine that its precedents "gave public officials the power to deny use of a forum in advance,"[29] providing adequate procedural safeguards were established.

In failing to distinguish the nature of various forms of expression, the public forum approach also disregards the varying degrees of protection the Court has applied in its press clause and public forum interpretation. Proponents suggest, for instance, that the college press "enjoy[s] the same protection from interference by administrators as is enjoyed by others who exercise their right to free expression in other public forums.[30] However, the Court has distinguished those standards which are most stringent where conduct is least involved. The press function is mostly conduct-free and stands in a preferred position, as in *Near,* while protection for the conduct-involved expression at issue in public forum cases, such as speech and association, are subject to time, place, and manner restrictions "in relation to the other proper uses"[31] of the forum.

Similarly, the standards imposed in public forum cases have varied with the type of activity considered. For example, the Court held in *Papish* that denial of access to its grounds for distribution of literature would require no less than constitutionally-defined obscenity[32] but held in *Widmar v. Vincent* that expression involving mere conduct, such as assembly, could be regulated by "reasonable campus rules."[33] Thus, while it is only the constitutionality of the content of press expression which is at issue, restriction of expression in the public forum must consider the form of expression as well as its content. The single purpose analysis of the Court's press clause cases has resulted in consistently higher standards than the dual purpose analysis of its public forum cases. Application of the latter rather than the former standards, then, unconstitutionally abridges college press freedom.

The public forum approach also presumes that college press is a traditional public forum. One of its advocates has argued, for instance, "school papers are like *other publicly owned places* that have been dedicated as forums where citizens can go and engage in the free exchange of ideas,"[34] using the example of parks. Another has asserted in the college press context that the central principle in the public forum doctrine is that "once the government creates a *forum for public expression,* its regulation of the forum must be consistent with first amendment guarantees.[35] Such analysis fails to recognize either that the Court's public forum theory was developed principally in addressing expressive uses of forums established primarily for other purposes or that it has distinguished between public and nonpublic forums.[36]

For instance, the Court overturned a prohibition on picketing on public streets as consistent with intended use of a forum but approved a similar restriction at a shopping center where such use was not related to the purpose of the forum.[37] Similarly, the Court refused to allow a school system to distinguish among teachers who could speak at a school board meeting, a public forum,[38] but allowed such a distinction regarding use of a school's mail boxes, a nonpublic forum.[39] Thus, the public forum approach inappropriately applies to college newspapers standards developed for providing expressive use of traditional public forums, such as streets and parks, and fails to heed the Court's warning that those standards should be applied "in light of the purpose which the forum serves."[40]

In addition, the approach presumes that college publications have been necessarily established as public forums and that the standards for regulation of conduct-related expression should be applied, instead of recognizing that they have been established as nonpublic forums for which the standards developed by the Court for regulating conduct-free expression are more appropriate. Such a distinction was suggested, for instance, when Justice Douglas agreed with restricting advertising card space on a public bus, since it was "more akin to a newspaper than a park,"[41] but would have found that a municipal theater was no less a public forum than a public park or sidewalk.[42]

Three other interrelated presumptions made by the public forum approach address the state's ownership of the college press. The first is that because the state owns the forum, the users of that forum become state agents themselves, whose actions also are subject to constitutional restriction. As one advocate of the approach phrased it, "the decisions of student editors constitute state action."[43] The second is unless the public forum approach and its focus on government action is used, "school officials would be 'publishers' with the power to control the content of the government-created publication in the same way that private publishers exercise control over commercial newspapers."[44]

Those presumptions, however, not only lead to constitutionally unacceptable implications, but incorrectly interpret public forum theory developed in the Court and are contradictory as well. The contradiction is apparent — if student editors are state agents, then they are subject to control by the state; if they are not subject to control by the state, then they are not state agents. The first presumption is supported by no suggestion in the Court's public forum cases that those who speak, march, or picket in the streets, parks, or any other public forums become state agents through the exercise of their rights. Both presumptions also fail to recognize that the First Amendment allows the state to define the forum and uses of its public forums, as the courts in several college press cases have noted.[45] Not only would it be consistent with public forum theory, then, for schools to establish student publications as nonpublic forums whose editors could exercise authority based on the editorial discretion model, but any government interference with that exercise would constitute an unconstitutional abridgement under the press clause.

Those presumptions also lead to a third, "necessary corollary to the forum theory," described as "a right of access to the student press by individuals other than the newspaper's editors and staffers."[46] That corollary relies on the questionable presumption that state action is inherent in the decision of the student editor and is constitutionally inadquate in any case: Whether or not the student editor is a state actor, his exercise of editorial discretion is protected by the press clause. That principle was succinctly stated by the Court of Appeals for the Ninth Circuit in *Associates & Aldrich Co., Inc. v. Times Mirror Co.:* "Even if state action were present, as in an official publication of a state-supported university, there is still the freedom to exercise subjective editorial discretion in rejecting a preferred article.[47] It also was the holding of *Lehman,* where denial of access was state action;[48] of *Columbia Broadcasting System, Inc. v. Democratic National Committee* and *FCC v. League of Women Voters,* where the medium had some government ties;[49] and of *Miami Herald Publishing Co. v. Tornillo,* where access did not involve state action.[50]

The public forum approach fails, finally, because it does not distinguish among and does not adequately prioritize the values underlying the clauses of the First Amendment as interpreted by the Supreme Court. For instance, one advocate of the public forum approach implied that free press rights were subsumed in the more general free speech rights, concluding "the student *press* . . . is now seen as enjoying the same freedom from regulation afforded by other *speech* activity in a public forum."[51] Another review of student press law[52] using the public forum approach asserted that the function of that press was to serve the marketplace value associated with the more general provisions for freedom of expression:

> Certainly, the student press plays a role in the closed society of a school not unlike the role its counterpart plays in society at large: Its mission should be to provide a forum for members of the school community to voice their opinions about issues of concern.

This interpretation of the function of the press and the First Amendment values it serves leads to the assertion that "long-suffering First Amendment principles governing control of public forum likewise govern the permissible regulation of student expression,"[53] including the college press. The preference for those principles reflects a preference for the values underlying the non-press clauses of the First Amendment, which "would bring the law of the student press into harmony with the public forum doctrine and the more general first amendment principles enunciated by the Supreme Court."[54]

Those values, however, threaten other First Amendment values represented by the Court's interpretation of the press clause, values which "are well established in Federal decisions dealing with the freedom of the press,"[55] as a federal judge in Mississippi put it:

> . . . the undoubted right to exercise an editorial judgment on what to put in and what not to put in the paper. *That is a freedom that belongs to the press of America.* How they exercise that right is up to those who publish printed material, free of judicial control. The First Amendment protects them specifically in their decision-making about what to print.[56]

As that judge noted in concluding that "the idea that a newspaper is like a public utility, that it must serve all comers if it serves any, has been completely rejected,[57] the conflict between those First Amendment rights has been resolved by the Supreme Court in *Tornillo:* "It has yet to be demonstrated how government regulation of this crucial process [of editorial control and judgment] can be exercised consistent with First Amendment guarantees of a free press."[58]

The theoretical foundation of the public forum approach fails, then, because it seeks to use government control of the press as a means to another First Amendment end, one which is laudable but neither supersedes nor subsumes the function served by the press. Meiklejohn has observed that "what is essential is not that everyone shall speak, but that everything worth saying shall be said."[59] That observation might serve as a fitting epitaph for the public forum approach to constitutional interpretation of the college press under the First Amendment, which seeks to achieve the less essential at the expense of the more essential. As the Court said in *Tornillo*, "A reasonable press is an undoubtedly desirable goal, but press responsibility is not mandated by the Constitution and, like many other virtues, it cannot be legislated."[60]

Editorial Discretion:
A Constitutional Approach to the College Press

The public forum and editorial discretion approaches to interpreting the college press under the First Amendment originated in 1967 in the first two college press cases which addressed its unique ownership circumstances. The former concept was developed early and can be identified in fourteen of the nineteen college press cases decided through 1975. In the last nine years, however, courts have relied on the later concept in six of the seven decisions, an indication that the lower courts have recognized it as a more appropriate approach, one which adequately extends to the college press the guarantees of the First Amendment against government interference with expression. That conclusion also is suggested by several other considerations.

First, those courts using the editorial discretion approach have neither distinguished nor suggested that the college press should be distinguished from the commercial press in defining its functions under and applying to it the standards and values of the press clause. Where prior restraint or subsequent punishment has been imposed, the college press has stood in the same preferred position—defined by the stringent nature of the tests applied—occupied by the commercial press.

Second, the values served by application of the editorial discretion concept are the same values which the Supreme Court has identified as underlying the press clause. Both the college and commercial press earn their First Amendment protection by serving the press clause–guaranteed functions of providing the information and criticism needed for self-government and community security through checking government abuse of official authority.

Third, because it does not distinguish between the roles played by the college press and the commercial press—and, therefore, through application of the same constitutional standards implies that they exercise the same educational model. As Trager has noted, implicitly recognizing the distinctive function of the press clause, "Freedom of expression and freedom of press are nowhere more important and worthy of defense than in colleges and universities."[61] The experience of the Reveille Seven demon-

CHAPTER 13   THEORIES FOR FREEDOM OF THE PRESS   **143**

strates that educational values suffer when education by example does not conform to education by ideal. That was the concern which motivated the press clause response of the court in *Klahr v. Winterble* to its observation that "the systems of politics and news media [on campus] are so obviously patterned after the situation off campus."⁶²

The editorial discretion approach also provides a starting point for unifying treatment of various segments of the college press under the First Amendment. First, by focusing on the state action involved in campus administrative censorship rather than the relationship of the administration to the publication, the concept eliminates discrimination on the public campus between three of the extracurricular models—authoritarian, student activity, and adviser—and the fourth, the independence model. Second, recognition of its educational value may commend it to educators in laboratory model publications: As the Court emphasized in *West Virginia State Board of Education v. Barnett,* "educating the young for citizenship is the reason for scrupulous protection of Constitutional freedoms of the individual."⁶³ Third, its focus upon the function of the press, particularly upon its service as a watchdog of the government of the community it serves, suggests that it might serve as a basis for reexamining the relationship between the government and the press on the private campus.

College student publications on public and private campuses are similar in all respects but one: Administrators at the former are state agents, and at the latter are not. Because of that distinction, few private college journalists have taken their demands for press freedom to the courts—none of the reported college press cases was initiated because of that issue. Ingelhart has suggested that private college students are reluctant to submit their case to the judiciary because of "an oft stated view that the courts would automatically reject press freedom since the First Amendment does not restrain private officials."⁶⁴ As the Supreme Court noted in another context in *CBS, Inc.,* however, "when government action is alleged there must be cautious analysis of the quality and degree of Government relationship to the particular acts in question."⁶⁵ Perhaps the editorial discretion concept, as a core mechanism in a preferred function guaranteed by the press clause of the First Amendment, can bring a fresh perspective to the caution with which the courts have assessed the public function of the private university, at least regarding its relationship with its student press: Where the First Amendment nexus between that government and that press is concerned, another assessment of whether the private university is "the functional equivalent of a municipality"⁶⁶ should be undertaken.

It has been noted that "private schools are considered vital parts of America's pluralistic society because they provide a diversity that government cannot always provide."⁶⁷ A relationship which violates the spirit of the Constitution in one of its crucial functions, however, poorly serves educational diversity and in doing so gravely imperils a principal educational goal at all institutions, preparing students for citizenship in a democratic society. By failing to distinguish the private college as publisher because of the governmental role it principally performs on the campus, private institutions are setting for their students a constitutionally bad example: Censorship by government, whether or not it is colored by law as state action, should be abhorred as an aberration and not defended as a norm.

Justice Douglas wrote in *CBS, Inc.* that it was "anathema to the First Amendment to allow Government any role of censorship over newspapers, magazines, books, art, music, TV, radio, or any other aspect of the press."[68] He also indicated in *Lehman* that the command of the First Amendment was not altered by the public or private nature of the press. If the courts were to eliminate such a distinction for college governments where they interfere with those college press functions which represent core First Amendment values, it would be a major step toward achieving a First Amendment theory for the college press which would prevent the dismissal or other punishment of any other student journalists "for practicing what we were being taught."

Dr. Reed's views stimulate a curiosity of just what the forum theory might involve. Most recent basic legal definition of the forum appeared in *Cornelius* v. *NAACP Legal Defense and Educational Fund.*[69] It pointed out that there are three distinct types of public forums.

First is an open public forum, which traditionally means that any person or member of the public may use it freely for expressive purposes.

Second is a limited public forum, which traditionally consists primarily of government property that has been opened for use as a place of expressive activities for a limited time. The Court has recognized that people generally have a First Amendment right to engage in expressive activity upon the property. The government's acquiescence in the use of the property as a forum for expressive activity tells us that such activity is compatible with the normal uses of the place.

Third is a nonpublic forum. Control over access to a nonpublic forum can be based upon subject matter and speaker identity so long as the distinctions are reasonable in light of the purpose served by the forum and the distinctions are viewpoint neutral on the part of the government.

The strength of the forum theory is that it establishes a theoretical basis for freedom of content on or in the property of the government, even in student publications owned by a public college. Weakness in the theory results from the ease of confusing which of the three kinds of forums might be applicable, confusion about official policies proclaiming the forum to be a forum or the demonstration of the forum being established by tradition or governmental acquiescence, and confusion about who controls viewpoint content or how diverse viewpoints must be. Courts must have evidence presented for each of these factors.

In actual litigation it appears that student plaintiffs (or defendants) should be prepared to argue and prove

- The student editor is the individual exercising protected and guaranteed First Amendment rights.
- The student editor is not an agent of the state under terms of the Fourteenth Amendment.
- The student editor is exercising routine protected editorial discretion.
- The content is fully protected expression under terms of the First Amendment.
- Student readers of the student publication are entitled to receive and read this content as part of their First Amendment rights.
- The university has officially proclaimed that the student publication provides freedom of expression for students.
- The university has accepted for a long time the practice of free expression maintained by the publication.

Not only does the First Amendment protect the freedom of the student press, but so do state constitutions. A state constitution may have guarantees even stronger than the United States Constitution and might prevail.

Certainly, competent attorneys should consider this multiple approach to litigation. Many case decisions provide precedents and successful arguments. Perhaps most important would be arguing that a vigorous student publication discussing matters of import is a highly desirable academic function of a modern university.

CHAPTER 14

Let's Be Sensible

Estimates indicate there are about 3,000 campus student newspapers, 2,000 yearbooks, 1,800 magazines, and 800 other student publications being regularly produced on about 3,600 higher education campuses. The student publications are diverse in appearance, content, and function, as were the institutions. In addition, there are at least several hundred student-managed radio and television stations.

College administrators, trustees, faculty members, and students in these institutions are continuing to search for ways to maintain and improve every facet of campus life and activity.[1] This search goes on because no one has yet claimed perfection for any campus or procedure.

Independence for the media—print or broadcast—is not automatically a helpful word or concept when applied to the campus student press. In the comprehensive survey conducted by College Media Advisers 548 colleges (68 percent) simply did not consider the campus newspaper to be independent of the college (251 or 32 percent did). The yearbook was not considered independent in 469 colleges (74 percent), while 158 (26 percent) of the colleges considered the book to be independent. An examination of data supplied by the colleges listing 409 publications considered independent indicates that only in 2 universities (Harvard and Yale) might publications be characterized as independent in terms of the criteria listed in Chapter 3. Thus, the independent college student press simply does not exist in the United States to any significant degree. Little can be gained by talking as if it did or could or should.

Instead, much more intelligent understanding and planning can evolve from a sensible and reasonable discussion based on data reflecting accurately the status of the campus student press.

For example, one survey said that 206 boards of trustees of colleges and universities have adopted official statements relative to freedom of the student press as it pertains to students of the institutions and student publications. But more than 600 college boards have not done so according to the College Media Advisers study. Although some student journalists fear that their boards would pass repressive statements, the general posture of statements adopted by boards has been substantially to endorse and provide for freedom of the campus press.

Freedom of the campus press does not mean independence from the university. Freedom of the campus press can be best characterized as a situation in which *students can publish without having to obtain prior approval from university officials.* Data presented earlier in this book indicated that the standard practice in American colleges is to provide for this situation.

Fiscal and financial arrangements, whether incorporated or not, should have no direct bearing on the freedom of the campus press in America—philosophically, practically, or legally.

John Ciardi, writing almost three decades ago in the *Saturday Review,* believed a sensible approach to student publications could be found in the Tufts College plan. He believed this plan should be "compulsory reading for all college and university administrators who have serious intent as educators."[2] Here is some of its official wording:

> It sometimes happens that the disproportions of student writing, as they spring onto the page from the unmanaged or half-managed compulsions of the writer, offend the more literal and less venturesome attitudes of the community. It can follow then that the "image" of the University will suffer in the eyes of the community; particularly so since this difference between the language-intoxicated young seeker and the more stable community around him is one that can be readily distorted to sensationalism by rumor and journalism. . . .
>
> Unless we are prepared to defend him [the young writer] at those times when his compulsion toward the honesty of his vision, no matter how mismanaged, brings him into conflict with the more sedate views of the community, we cannot wish him well in his seeking, nor can we fulfill our purposes as a University.
>
> The University, therefore, will not act as a censor. The right to publish student and other writings is vested in the principal editor of each of the three student publications and three faculty advisers whose decision is subject to no revision by the University. These editors and advisers have been chosen in good faith and we cannot fail to believe that they will act in

good faith. It is the University policy, moreover, that in case of a tie vote the final decision shall rest with the student editor.

The University is aware that a decision so reached may not be the decision the faculty and the administration would have reached. It is even conceivable that a decision so reached may be embarrassing to the University. Freedom, however, must include not only the freedom to choose, but the freedom to make honest mistakes when personal conviction is at stake. The University believes that its enduring function is better served by freedom than by censorship.

Ciardi, of course, was known as a person of letters, but Dr. Annette Gibbs was not. She was associate dean of students at the University of Virginia in Charlottesville when she proposed a set of guidelines for college student publications.[3] Having studied reports and statements from a wide variety of organizations, she proposed these guidelines:

1. The function of the college student newspaper should be clearly defined and agreed on by the students, faculty, and administrators within the college community.

2. The function of the college student newspaper, as it is related to student freedom of expression, is parallel with the function of the commercial newspaper, i.e., to inform, educate, and entertain their readers.

3. The student newspaper should not be considered as an official publication of the college or university.

4. Students attending state colleges and universities do not forfeit their constitutional rights of freedom of expression.

5. Private colleges and universities traditionally have maintained constitutional independence in that they have been free to censor student publications; however, this private corporate status may now be challenged because of the vast amounts of federal and state funding that these institutions are receiving.

6. Student newspaper editorial policies that promote the lawful educational goals of the college or university are viewed as desirable by the courts.

7. A publications board, composed of students, faculty, and administrators, offers the best method for providing guidance and leadership for the college student newspaper activity.

8. Student newspaper editorial freedom of expression requires student responsibility for presenting news and opinion accurately, fairly, and completely.

9. A professionally competent adviser for the student newspaper staff is desirable for both students and the college administration.

10. The college student newspaper is primarily a medium of com-

munication for students; other opportunities made possible for students who participate in newspaper activities, such as formal course instruction in writing and technical skills, are secondary.

Both Ciardi and Gibbs were asking for a sensible, realistic approach to the campus student press.

It is clear that no single student publication plan can be prescribed for all American colleges. Indeed, it is certain that a dozen or so basic plans could be suggested—but an exceptional plan by a college could surpass any of these patterns in terms of effectiveness. Several generalizations can be drawn, however.

1. The campus student press is a firmly established and accepted part of American higher education.

2. By law and by precept, the campus student press should be published with no requirement for prior approval of content by the university.

3. Each college and university should arrange for a student newspaper and a yearbook. A campus student magazine would also be advisable. Size and frequency of these publications would vary with the diversity of universities and colleges.

4. The board of trustees should adopt a general policy statement indicating its support of a free campus student press and defining the relationship of the publications to the university.

5. A board of publications, including adequate membership by student staff members and advisers, should develop the statement accepted as university policy by the board of trustees and additional policy guidelines for the publications. This board would thus be a policy agency and not a supervising or administrative board.

6. Each student publication staff should have a qualified adviser, preferably a member of the journalism faculty.

7. Adequate instruction in journalism skills and concepts should be made available to student staff members. Preferably this should be accomplished through an academic journalism program.

8. A student publication could be organized as a student club, or as an administrative unit, an auxiliary enterprise, or as a nonprofit corporation. If the corporate arrangement is utilized, the articles of incorporation should indicate clearly the relationship of the publication to the university. Generally, student publications should be related structurally to the journalism instructional program.

9. A stable and adequate plan for financing each student publication should be devised. The most efficient and economical plan would

include an allocation from student fees or other university funds. Most student publications should utilize other sources, particularly advertising. Whimsical antagonisms of student government cannot be allowed to manipulate fee allocation levels to the publications. The fee allocation should be high enough to provide copies of newspapers, yearbooks, or magazines to all students wanting them without additional charge. Publications should be entitled to sell subscriptions to nonstudents; on most campuses subscription sales to students is far too inefficient a plan to provide sufficient financial stability for student publications. Fund allocations should be at a level sufficient to cover from one-third to one-half the budget of the newspaper, one-half to two-thirds the budget of the yearbook, and two-thirds to all the budget of a magazine. Thus the newspaper or yearbook or magazine would need additional revenue from such areas as advertising, printing, photographic services, space charges, or others.

10. Student publications generally should not be associated structurally with student government.

11. Careful study of each college and each of its student publications would be necessary before reliable advice for structuring the student publications program could be recommended. This is especially true for any plans for incorporation. College Media Advisers, Inc., can recommend excellent consultants.

12. Each student publications adviser should be an active member of CMA.

13. Whenever financially feasible, adequate production equipment should be available on campus for each publication to use. This may mean that full-time technical, bookkeeping, and clerical persons would need to be employed by large student publications. An on-campus offset printing press is also desirable for some student publications.

14. The faculty adviser is logically the person best able to conduct the fiscal management functions normally accomplished by an individual serving as publisher. The adviser can be the rallying person providing for the continuity and traditions of each publication. In no case would adviser service extend to editorial or content control; nor would the adviser be allowed to approve content prior to publication.

15. College presidents should not fear that the student publications might publish offensive material. College students are sophisticated beyond shock or stampede. Instead the college president should seize the public relations initiative and responsibility by telling the simple truth: by law, the student press is free; philosophically, the university has endorsed a free student press as desirable; and the content of the publications does not represent the position, preference, or performance of

the university, its staff, or its students generally.

16. The student publication should be urged to carry a statement in each issue indicating that it speaks only for the student members of its staff and not for other students of the university.

17. The student publications should be encouraged to accept diverse opinions of nonstaff students for publications.

18. Adequate housing and facilities should be available to each student publication on campus.

19. Student publishing efforts other than the newspaper, yearbook, and magazine should be free to proceed without administrative interferences. If the newspaper, yearbook, and magazine are able to function well there will be surprisingly few efforts for so-called underground publications to develop. If they do, however, no efforts should be made to stop them.

20. If enough students take enough journalism classes taught by enough qualified journalism teachers, students will produce well-written and well-edited publications. If ideal combinations of the above are not available, informal training efforts should be organized.

These 20 precepts give valid advice for any university in its student publications program. They will not eliminate all problems, but they will establish an atmosphere for sensible operations. They will help make possible lively, widely read, well-written, and well-edited student publications.

And more importantly they ask the university community to recognize, endorse, and live with a vigorous free press. Perhaps no more important or needed lesson can be learned or taught in American colleges and universities in this century.

Reliable information and resource materials can be found readily in the following sources.

Books

The College Media Directory, 1989. New York: Oxbridge Communications, 1989. This title replaces the old title of *Directory of the College Student Press in America* for its 1986 and earlier editions. Dario Politella, consulting editor for the 1989 *Directory,* reports that it lists 2,443 newspapers, 1,474 yearbooks, and 1,358 magazines on 3,692 campuses. The biggest change was the increase of 109 yearbooks containing an average of 5.5 more pages per book in 1989 over 1986.[4] Apparently there are more than 2,000 faculty advisers serving student publications in at least 1,300 colleges.

Ethics and Responsibilities of Advising College Student Publications.

Kopenhaver and Click. Memphis, TN: College Media Publications, Department of Journalism, Memphis State University, 1978.
Excellence in College Journalism. Overbeck and Pasqua. Belmont, CA: Wadsworth, 1983.
The First Amendment Handbook. Jane E. Kirtley, ed. Washington, DC: The Reporters Committee for Freedom of the Press.
Freedom for the College Student Press. Louis E. Ingelhart. Westport, CT: Greenwood Press, 1985.
Governing College Student Publications. J. William Click. Memphis, TN: College Media Advisers, 1985.
Law of the Student Press. Student Press Law Center. Iowa City, IA: University of Iowa, Quill and Scroll, School of Journalism and Mass Communications, 1988.
Student Press in America Archives. New York: Utica College, 1950–.
Synopsis of the Law of Libel and the Right of Privacy (2nd rev. ed.). New York: Sanford, Scripps-Howard Newspapers, World Almanac Publications, 1984.

Periodicals

College Media Law Review. CMA Headquarters, Department of Journalism, Memphis State University, Memphis, TN 38152.
The Collegiate Journalist. Society of Collegiate Journalists, Institute of Journalism, CBN University, Virginia Beach, VA 23450.
News Media and the Law. Reporters Committee for Freedom of the Press, Suite 504, 1735 Eye St., N.W., Washington, DC 20006.
Quill. Society of Professional Journalists, 53 W. Jackson, Suite 731, Chicago, IL 60604.
Report. Student Press Law Center, Suite 504, 1735 Eye St., N.W., Washington, DC 20006.
Right to Know. Gannet News Service, FOI Box, 1627 K St. N.W., Washington, DC 20006.

Charters of Incorporation

The following incorporation charters were in effect during the 1988–89 academic year. Incorporated student publications staff members, advisers, and managers are indeed an enthusiastic and helpful group of persons who are proud of the achievements of publications that are usually considered to be of excellent quality. These persons would be supportive and helpful to a publications staff considering incorporation. A phone call, a letter, or a visit would bring help and advice.

Articles of Incorporation
IOWA STATE DAILY
November 5, 1980

Article I. The name of the Corporation is the IOWA STATE DAILY PUBLICATION BOARD, INC. Said Corporation is the successor to the IOWA STATE DAILY STUDENT PUBLICATION BOARD.

Article II. The period of its duration is perpetual.

Article III.

A. The business, objects and purposes for which this Corporation is formed are to publish and sell the Iowa State University student newspaper, known as the "Iowa State Daily" as a means of promoting the educational welfare of and providing business and editorial experience for those students who participate in the enterprise. Said Corporation may solicit and receive gifts, grants of money and property of every kind, and administer the same for educational purposes and do everything necessary or proper for the accomplishment of these purposes.

B. The Corporation is organized and shall be operated both for educational purposes and business and editorial experience, all for the public welfare, and no part of the net earnings of the Corporation shall inure to the benefit of any private member of the Corporation.

Article IV. The address of the initial registered office of the Corporation in the State of Iowa is 129 Press Building, Iowa State University, in the City of Ames, County of Story, and the name of its initial registered agent at such address is Robert Greenlee.

Article V. The affairs of the Corporation shall be managed by the Publication Board. Two members of the Board shall be voting faculty members. Any others deemed necessary shall be ex-officio. The Publication Board shall have general charge of the business and affairs of the Corporation, including the power to adopt by-laws. The names and addresses of the persons who are to serve as the initial members of the Publication Board are: [names omitted]. Members of the Publication Board, with the exception of the faculty members, must be students at Iowa State University in good standing and selected as provided in the by-laws. Membership shall cease upon selection of a successor or successors as provided in the by-laws or upon graduation, voluntary resignation, or loss of good standing as a student at Iowa State University. Membership of any member may be terminated by a three-fourths vote of all members of the Publication Board.

Article VI. The Corporation shall have no members other than the Publication Board as hereinbefore provided.

Article VII. The Corporation may be dissolved at any regular or special meeting by an affirmative vote of three-fourths or more of the members of the Publication Board. In the event of liquidation, dissolution or winding up of the Corporation, whether voluntary, involuntary or by operation of law, any disposition made of the assets of the Corporation shall be such as is calculated exclusively to carry out the objects and purposes for which the Corporation is formed.

Article VIII. Except for this Article and Article VII which require a vote of three-fourths or more of the members of the Publication Board, these Articles of Incorporation may be amended by a majority vote of the Publication Board members present in person or by proxy at any annual or special meeting called for that purpose, providing a notice of the proposed amendment and the substance thereof be sent to all members of the Publication Board at least ten (10) days prior to the date for such meeting.

University of Kentucky
Articles of Incorporation of
THE KERNEL PRESS, INC.
1971

We, the undersigned natural persons of the age of eighteen years or more, acting as incorporators of a corporation under the Kentucky Non-profit Corporation Act (Chapter 273 of the Kentucky Revised Statutes) adopt the following Articles of Incorporation for such corporation.

FIRST: The name of the corporation is The Kernel Press, Inc.

SECOND: The corporation is to have perpetual existence.

THIRD: The exclusive purpose for which the corporation is formed is the promotion of educational skill and the publication and distribution of a collegiate newspaper in and about the University of Kentucky. The said newspaper or newspapers shall be printed and published at the City of Lexington, State of Kentucky and at such other place or places as the corporation may deem advisable.

FOURTH: The conditions and regulations of membership and the rights or other privileges of the classes of members shall be determined and fixed by the bylaws.

FIFTH: In the event of the dissolution of this corporation, the assets thereof, after payment of all obligations, shall be transferred to the University of Kentucky for the purpose of providing scholarships for students in the Journalism Department at that institution.

SIXTH: The address of the initial registered office of the corporation is 1272 Priscilla Lane, Lexington, Kentucky . . . and the name of its initial registered agent is: [name omitted]

SEVENTH: The number of directors constituting the initial Board of Directors of the corporation is thirteen and they are to serve as directors until the first annual meeting of the members or until their successors are elected and shall qualify. [Names omitted.]

EIGHTH: The names and addresses of three incorporators are: [names omitted].

NINTH: The corporation shall have power:

(1) To have perpetual succession by its corporate name.

(2) To sue and be sued, complain and defend the corporate name.

(3) To have a corporate seal and alter it at pleasure, provided, however, that the presence or absence of a corporate seal on or from a writing shall neither add to nor detract from the legality thereof nor affect its validity in any manner or respect.

(4) Subject to the provisions of KRS 273.383 to purchase, take, receive, lease, take by gift, devise or bequest, or otherwise acquire, own, hold, improve, use and otherwise deal in and with real or personal property, or any interest therein, wherever situated.

(5) To sell, convey, mortgage, pledge, lease, exchange, transfer and otherwise dispose of all or any part of its property and assets.

(6) To lend money to its employees other than its officers and directors and otherwise assist its employees.

(7) To purchase, take, receive, subscribe for, or otherwise acquire, own, hold, vote, use, employ, sell, mortgage, lend, pledge, or otherwise dispose of, and otherwise use and deal in and with, shares or other interests in, or obligations of, other domestic or foreign corporations, whether for profit or not for profit, associations, partnerships or individuals, or direct or indirect on ligations of the United States, or of any other government, state, territory, governmental district or municipality or of any instrumentality thereof.

(8) To make contracts and incur liabilities, borrow money at such rates of interest as the corporation may determine, issue its notes, bonds, and other obligations, and secure any of its obligations by mortgage or pledge of all or any of its property, franchises and income.

(9) To lend money for investment, to invest its funds, and take and hold real and personal property as security for the payment of funds so loaned or invested.

(10) To conduct its affairs, carry on its operations, have offices and exercise the powers granted by KRS 273.161 to 273.383 in any state, territory, district, or possession of the United States, or in any foreign country.

(11) To elect or appoint officers and agents of the corporation, who may be directors or members, and define their duties and fix their compensation.

(12) To make and alter bylaws, not inconsistent with these Articles of Incorporation or with the laws of this state, for the administration and regulation of the affairs of the corporation.

(13) To make donations for the public welfare or for charitable, scientific or educational purposes.

(14) To indemnify any director or officer or former director or officer of the corporation, or any person who may have served at its request as a director or officer of another corporation in which it owns share of capital stock or of which it is a creditor, against expenses actually and reasonably incurred by him in connection with the defense of any action, suit or proceeding, civil or criminal, in which he is made a party by reason of being or having been such director or officer, except in relation to matters as to which he shall be adjudged in such action, suit or proceeding to be liable for negligence or misconduct in the performance of duty to the corporation; and to make any other indemnification that shall be authorized by the Articles of Incorporation or bylaws, or resolution adopted after notice to the members entitled to vote.

(15) To pay pensions and insurance plans for any or all of the directors, officers and employees.

(16) To cease its corporate activities and surrender its corporate franchise.

(17) To have and exercise all powers necessary or convenient to effect any or all of the purposes for which the corporation is organized.

Articles of Incorporation of
MARYLAND MEDIA, INC.
October 1971

THIS IS TO CERTIFY:

FIRST: That we, the subscribers, Buddy Brown, c/o Student Government Association, University of Maryland, College Park, Maryland; Michael Dolan, 9223 Baltimore Boulevard, College Park, Maryland; Andrew Sharp, c/o Department of Journalism, University of Maryland, College Park, Maryland, all being of full legal age, do, under and by virtue of the laws of the State of

Maryland authorizing the formation of corporations, associate ourselves with the intention of forming a corporation.

SECOND: The name of the corporation (which is hereinafter called the "corporation") is:

MARYLAND MEDIA, INC.

THIRD: The purposes for which the corporation is formed and the objects to be carried on and performed by it are as follows:

(a) To edit, print, publish, sell and distribute those student publications for the University of Maryland as the corporation shall determine as an educational, informational and literary service independent of but in harmony with the University of Maryland community;

(b) To obtain professional publishing expertise to advise student editors of the publications at the College Park Campus of the University of Maryland;

(c) To do all other lawful acts necessary and proper to the accomplishment of these foregoing purposes.

(d) No part of the net earnings of the corporation shall inure to the benefit of any director, officer or member of the corporation, or any private individual (except that reasonable compensation may be paid for services rendered to or for the corporation effecting one or more of its purposes), and no director, officer, or member of the corporation, or any private individual shall be entitled to share in the distribution of any of the corporate assets on dissolution of the corporation. No substantial part of the activities of the corporation shall be the carrying on of propaganda, or otherwise attempting, to influence legislation, and the corporation shall not participate in, or intervene in (including the publication or distribution of statements) any political campaign on behalf of any candidate for public office.

(e) The corporation is organized solely for educational and literary purposes and only in furtherance of those purposes will the corporation carry out the activities set forth in this certificate, and the corporation shall not conduct or carry on any activities not permitted to be conducted or carried on by an organization exempt under Section 501(c)(3) of the Internal Revenue Code and its Regulations as they now exist or as they may hereafter be amended, or by an organization's contributions to which are deductible under Section 170(c)(2) of such Code and Regulations as they now exist or as they may hereafter be amended.

(f) Upon the dissolution of the corporation or the winding up of its affairs, the assets of the corporation shall be distributed exclusively for the educational, informational and literary benefit of the students at the University of Maryland, College Park Campus, and only for purposes exempt under Section 501(c)(3) of the Internal Revenue Code.

(g) As a means of accomplishing the foregoing purposes the corporation shall have the following powers:

1. To accept, acquire, receive, take and hold by bequest, devise, grant,

gift, purchase, exchange, lease, transfer, by judicial order or by decree, or otherwise, for any of its objects and purposes, any property, both real and personal, of whatever kind, nature or description and wherever situated.

2. To sell, exchange, convey, mortgage, lease, transfer, or otherwise dispose of, any such property both real and personal, as the object and purposes of the corporation may require, subject to such limitations as may be prescribed by law.

3. To borrow and from time to time make, accept, endorse, execute and issue bonds, debentures, promissory notes, bills of exchange and other obligations of the corporation for monies borrowed or in payment for property acquired or for any of the other purposes of the corporation and to secure the payment of such obligations by mortgage, pledge, deed, indenture, agreement or other instrument of trust, or by other lien upon, assignment of, or agreement in regard to all or any part of the property, rights or privileges of the corporation wherever situated, whether now owned or hereafter to be acquired.

4. To invest and reinvest its funds in such stock, common or preferred, bonds, debentures, mortgages, or in such other securities and property as its Board of Directors shall deem advisable subject to the limitations and conditions contained in any bequest, devise, grant or gift provided with the provisions of Section 501(c)(3) of the Internal Revenue Code and its Regulations as they now exist or as they may hereafter be amended.

5. In general, and subject to such limitations and conditions as are or may be prescibed by law, to exercise such other powers which now are or hereafter may be conferred by law upon a corporation organized for the purposes hereinabove set forth, or necessary or incidental to the powers so conferred or conducive to the obtainment of the purposes of the corporation, subject to the further limitation and condition that, notwithstanding any other provisions of this certificate, only such powers shall be exercised as are in furtherance of the purposes of the corporation and as may be exercised by the organization exempt under Section 501(c)(3) of the Internal Revenue Code and its Regulations as they now exist or as they may hereafter be amended and by an organization, contributions to which are deductible under Section 170(c)(2) of such Code, and Regulations as they now exist or as they may hereafter be amended.

FOURTH: The territory in which the operations of the corporation are principally to be conducted is the United States of America, its territories and possessions, but the operations of the corporation shall not be limited to such territory.

FIFTH: The post office address at which the principal office of the corporation in this state will be located is: Department of Journalism, University of Maryland, College Park, Maryland. The resident agent of the corporation is Dr. Lee M. Brown whose post office address is: c/o Department of Journalism, University of Maryland, College Park, Maryland. Said resident agent is a citizen of the State of Maryland and actually resides therein.

SIXTH: The management and affairs of the corporation shall be vested in a Board of Directors. The Board of Directors may, by appropriate by-laws, amend the number of directors. The directors shall be authorized to fill vacancies in their number in the manner as directors at the first meeting of the corporation.

SEVENTH: The corporation shall have no capital stock and the members thereof shall consist of the members of the Board of Directors, and such persons thereafter who may from time to time be elected as directors. The corporation shall have no stockholders and is not organized for profit.

EIGHTH: The duration of the corporation shall be perpetual.

Michigan State University
(non-profit)
Articles of Incorporation
STATE NEWS

The Articles of Incorporation are signed and acknowledged by the incorporators for the purpose of forming a non-profit corporation under the provisions of Act No. 327 of the Public Acts of 1931, as amended, as follows:

ARTICLE I. The name of the corporation is *State News.*

ARTICLE II. The purpose or purposes for which the corporation is formed are as follows:

1. The publication, circulation and distribution of a student newspaper within the community of Michigan State University;

2. The assurance that both tone and content of such student newspaper are determined by the student editorial staff;

3. The prohibition of powers of veto and censorship over the news and editorial content thereof;

4. The acceptance of advice and criticism from administrators, faculty and students of Michigan State University who are not staff members of such newspaper.

ARTICLE III. The location of the first registered office is Student Services Building, East Lansing, Ingham (County), Michigan 48823. The post office address of the first registered office is Student Services Building, East Lansing, Ingham (County), Michigan 48823.

ARTICLE IV. The name of the first resident agent is Louis J. Berman.

ARTICLE V. Said corporation is organized upon a non-stock basis. The amount of assets which said corporation possesses is no real property and $100,000.00 in personal property. Said corporation is to be financed under the following general plan: gifts, subscriptions, receipts from advertising and sale of newspapers.

ARTICLE VI. The names and places of residence, or business, of three incorporators (and if a corporation is organized upon a stock-share basis the number of shares of stock subscribed for by each) are as follows: [names omitted].

ARTICLE VII. Seven persons are listed as the original Board of Directors.

ARTICLE VIII. The term of the corporate existence is perpetual.

ARTICLE IX. Membership in this corporation is strictly personal, and cannot be the subject of transfer, upon dissolution, assets remaining after payment of debts shall be transferred to the Board of Trustees of Michigan State University for educational purposes; and no part thereof shall inure to the benefit of any individual.

ARTICLE X. A volunteer director of the corporation shall not be personally liable to the corporation or its shareholders or members for monetary damages for a breach of the director's fiduciary duty arising under applicable law. However, this Article shall not eliminate or limit the liability of directors for any of the following:

(1) a breach of the director's duty of loyalty to the corporation or its shareholders or members,

(2) acts or omissions not in good faith or that involve intentional misconduct or knowing violation of law.

(3) a violation of Section 551 (1) of the Michigan Non-profit Corporation Act,

(4) a transaction from which the director derived an improper personal benefit,

(5) an act or omission occurring before January 1, 1988, or

(6) an act or omission that is grossly negligent.

A volunteer director of the corporation shall only be personally liable for monetary damages for a breach of fiduciary duty as a director to the corporation, its shareholders, or its members to the extent set forth in this Article X. Any repeal or modification of this Article X by the shareholders or members of the corporation shall not adversely affect any right or protection of any volunteer director of the corporation existing at the time of, or for or with respect to, any acts or omissions occurring before such repeal or modification. This Amendment shall be effective as of January 1, 1988.

Oklahoma State University
Amended Articles of Incorporation
of
THE O'COLLEGIAN PUBLISHING COMPANY
Stillwater, Oklahoma

KNOW ALL MEN BY THESE PRESENTS:

That we, whose names are hereunto subscribed, do hereby associate ourselves together for the purpose of forming a corporation under the provisions of the laws of the State of Oklahoma, and for that purpose state:

ARTICLE I. The name of this corporation shall be "The O'Collegian Publishing Company" of Stillwater, Oklahoma.

ARTICLE II. The purpose for which this corporation is formed to acquire, hold, and dispose of property for educational purposes and all be strictly confined to carrying out the objectives and purposes of the Oklahoma State University of Agriculture and Applied Science, Stillwater, Oklahoma, under the rules and regulations of the Board of Regents for the Oklahoma Agricultural and Mechanical Colleges and the President of said institution. This corporation shall manage the business affairs of the O'Collegian newspaper published on the campus of Oklahoma State University to include, but not limited to, the ordering of equipment, the payment of bills and obligations, the borrowing of money, and all other powers necessary for the efficient business operation of this corporation. It shall have as a further purpose the publication of the O'Collegian newspaper of Oklahoma State University.

ARTICLE III. The location of this corporation shall be at the Oklahoma State University of Agriculture and Applied Science, Stillwater, Payne County, Oklahoma.

ARTICLE IV. The term for which this corporation shall exist shall be perpetual.

ARTICLE V. There shall be seven (7) directors of this corporation, as follows: The President of Oklahoma State University of Agriculture and Applied Science, the Director of the Budget, the Director of the School of Journalism, the Dean of Student Affairs, the O'Collegian Editor, the Director of Student Publications, and the Chairman of the Board of Student Publications.

The officers of said Board of Directors being: [names omitted].

The said Board of Directors and said officers are to hold office until their successor is duly chosen under the Bylaws of this corporation as approved by the President.

ARTICLE VI. No part of the net earnings of the corporation shall inure to the benefit of, or be distributable to its members, trustees, officers, or other private persons, except that the corporation shall be authorized and empowered to pay reasonable compensation for services rendered and to make payments and distributions in furtherance of the purpose set forth in Article II hereof. No substantial part of the activities of the corporation shall be the carrying on of propaganda, or otherwise attempting, to influence furtherance of the purposes set forth in Article II hereof. No substantial part of the activities of the corporation shall be the carrying on of propaganda, or otherwise attempting, to influence legislation, and the corporation shall not participate in, or intervene in (including the publishing or distribution of statements) any political campaign on behalf of any candidate for public office. Notwithstanding any other provisions of these articles, the corporation shall not carry on any other activities not permitted to be carried on (a) by a corporation exempt from Federal income tax under section 501(c)(3) of the Internal Revenue Code of 1954 (or the corresponding provisions of any to which are deductible under section 170(c)(2) of the Internal Revenue Code of 1954 (or the corresponding provisions of any future United States Internal Revenue Law).

ARTICLE VII. Upon the dissolution of the corporation, the Board of Directors shall, after paying or making provisions for the payment of all the liabilities of the corporation exclusively for the purposes of the corporation in such manner, or to such organization or organizations organized and operated exclusively for charitable, educational, religious, or scientific purposes as shall at the time qualify as an exempt organization or organizations under section 501(c)(3) of the Internal Revenue Code of 1954 (or the corresponding provisions of any future United States Internal Revenue Law), as the Board of Directors shall determine. Any of such assets not so disposed of shall be disposed of by the District Court in which the principal office of the corporation is then located, exclusively for such purposes or to such organization or organizations, as said Court shall determine, which are organized and operated exclusively for such purpose.

ARTICLE VIII. All meetings of the Board of Directors shall be held on the campus of Oklahoma State University, Stillwater, Oklahoma.

ARTICLE IX. These Articles of Incorporation may be amended only by unanimous consent of the members at a meeting called for such purpose.

[The O'Collegian Publishing Company was first incorporated August 31, 1926.]

Articles of Incorporation of
PURDUE STUDENT PUBLISHING FOUNDATION

ARTICLE I. The name of this corporation shall be Purdue Student Publishing Foundation.

ARTICLE II. The purposes of this corporation shall be:

A. To promote and assist in the teaching and study of journalism, business and personnel administration, and advertising sales at Purdue University.

B. To edit, print, publish, and distribute at Purdue University a student newspaper, which shall be known as "THE PURDUE EXPONENT" and such other publications as the Board of Directors of the corporation shall determine appropriate and desirable.

ARTICLE III. In furtherance, and not in limitation of the general powers conferred by the laws of the State of Indiana and the common law, upon charitable foundations and corporations, and of the purposes and powers stated within, this corporation shall also have the following powers:

A. To contract for the printing and publishing of its publications.

B. To purchase, acquire, apply for, register, secure, hold, own, or sell copyrights, trademarks, and distinctive marks.

C. To purchase or otherwise acquire, own or hold real and personal property of every kind and description suitable, necessary, useful, or advisable in connection with any of the purposes of the corporation, and to sell, assign, convey, transfer, lease, mortgage, pledge, exchange or otherwise dispose of any such property and to make and enter into all contracts, agreements and obligations in any way necessary, useful or advisable to the effectuation of the purposes of the corporation as stated within.

D. The corporation may receive by gift, devise, bequest or otherwise, any money or property, absolutely or in trust, to be used, whether the principal or income therefrom, for the furtherance of any of the purposes of the corporation expressed within, or for any other purpose or purposes which may hereafter be or become within its corporate powers and objectives.

ARTICLE IV. The period during which it is to continue as a corporation is perpetual.

ARTICLE V. The post office address of its principal office is Purdue Memorial Union, West Lafayette, Indiana 47907.

ARTICLE VI. The membership of the corporation shall consist of the voting members of the Board of Directors. The business and affairs of the corporation shall be determined and managed by a Board of Directors consisting of thirteen (13) members divided into three (3) categories (classes) as follows:

A. Category (Class) A

Seven (7) members who shall be registered as full-fee students at the West Lafayette campus of Purdue University.

B. Category (Class) B

Three (3) members of the full-time regular faculty at the West Lafayette campus of Purdue University.

C. Category (Class) C

Three (3) members who shall come from the Greater Lafayette business and professional community.

ARTICLE VII. Ex-officio members of the Board of Directors shall be added to the Board of Directors as their services are required. The terms of such members shall be specified at the time of their appointments. The editor in chief, business manager, advertising director, advertising manager, production director, production manager, news staff director, and publisher shall all have ex-officio positions on the Board of Directors. All ex-officio positions shall be non-voting.

ARTICLE VIII. No members or directors of this corporation shall receive any pecuniary benefit, except reimbursement for expenses actually incurred or per diem allowances.

ARTICLE IX. In the event of the dissolution of this corporation, all of its property, real, personal and mixed, wherever situated, shall vest immediately and absolutely in the trustees of Purdue University to be used as financial aid for students attending Purdue University, and none of the property shall inure to the benefit of any director, member or employee of the corporation.

ARTICLE X. Amendments to these Articles shall be made only upon approval of nine (9) directors.

ARTICLE XI. The names and addresses of the incorporators are as follows: [names omitted].

NOTES

INTRODUCTION

1. John H. Schuh, *Enhancing Relationships with the Student Press* (San Francisco: Jossey-Bass, 1986).
2. David Knott, ed., *College Media Review* (Memphis, TN: College Media Advisers, 1975).
3. Julius Duscha and Thomas Fischer, *The Campus Press: Freedom and Responsibility* (Washington, DC: American Association of State Colleges and Universities, 1973).
4. Louis E. Ingelhart, *The College and University Student Press* (Memphis, TN: College Media Advisers, 1973).
5. George E. Stevens and John B. Webster, *Law and the Student Press* (Ames: Iowa State University Press, 1973).
6. Student Press Law Center, *Law of the Student Press* (Washington, DC: Student Press Law Center, 1988).
7. Louis E. Ingelhart, *Freedom for the College Student Press* (Westport, CT: Greenwood, 1985).

CHAPTER 1

1. Dario Politella, "Guidelines on the Freedoms and Responsibilities of the College Student Press in America," *Seminar,* December 1969 Supplement.
2. "Stanford Daily Goes Independent," *Editor and Publisher,* March 3, 1979, p. 20.
3. Fred M. Hechinger, "Cutting the Apron Strings," *New York Times,* October 15, 1972.
4. Noel Greenwood, "The Daily Cal Leaves Campus. Who's Next?" *Quill,* December 1971, pp. 14–15.
5. Perry D. Sorenson, "One Way to Get Rid of Racy College Papers," *National Observer,* January 13, 1973, p. 18.
6. "One Year Old; Alive and Well," *Kentucky Kernel,* December 13, 1972, p. 7.
7. "Senate Marches to O'Connell's," *Florida Alligator,* January 10, 1973, p. 1.
8. Teresa L. Ebert, "More Papers Cutting Ties with Colleges—but with Some Misgivings," *The Chronicle of Higher Education,* November 6, 1972, p. 5.
9. Julius Duscha, and Thomas Fischer, *The Campus Press. Freedom and Responsibility* (Washington, DC: American Association of State Colleges and Universities, 1973). References to this report will be indicated by page number in the text of that book.
10. The Washington Journalism Center is located at 2401 Virginia Ave-

nue, N.W., Washington, DC. It has been in operation since 1966. It provides fellowships for professional journalists and for black students interested in careers in journalism. It also arranges conferences on major issues in the news for journalists.

11. Melvin Mencher, *The College Press Review* 13, no.1 (Autumn 1973): pp. 16–20.

CHAPTER 2

1. Duscha and Fischer, *Campus Press.*
2. Sorenson, "One Way to Get Rid of Racy College Papers," p. 18.
3. *Heights* Restructuring Committee Report on Re-Structuring of the *Heights* Inc.
4. Duscha and Fischer, *Campus Press,* pp. 23–26.
5. Regents of the University of California and the Independent Berkeley Student Publishing Cooperative, University of California Agreement, October 1971.
6. Articles of Incorporation of the *Daily Californian* (A Non-Profit California Corporation), July 22, 1971.
7. Melvin Mencher, "Independence (by fiat) for the Campus Press," *Quill,* March 1973, p. 16.
8. Articles of Incorporation and Amendments thereto of the *Colorado Daily,* September 24, 1970.
9. Mencher, "Independence (by fiat)," pp. 14, 15.
10. Sorenson, "One Way to Get Rid of Racy College Papers," p. 18.
11. Ebert, "More Papers Cutting Ties," p. 5.
12. Ibid.
13. Sorenson, "One Way to Get Rid of Racy College Papers," p. 18.
14. Mencher, "Independence (by fiat)," p. 16.
15. Wendy Snyder, "O'Connell Announces Plan for Independence," *Florida Alligator,* January 10, 1973, p. 1.
16. Hechinger, "Cutting the Apron Strings."
17. Illini Publishing Company Charter Provisions and By-Laws, revised April 1, 1970.
18. Illini Publishing Company Charter Provisions and By-Laws.
19. Articles of Incorporation of the Kernel Press, Inc., October 1971.
20. Duscha and Fischer, *Campus Press,* pp. 32–34.
21. Article V, Section 4g, Student Governance, Marymount Manhattan College.
22. Ad Hoc Committee for Amendment of Article 6, *Academic Freedom Report for Students at Michigan State University.*
23. "Code of Ethics," Advertising and Editorial Handbook, *Michigan Daily.*
24. Sorenson, "One Way to Get Rid of Racy College Papers," p. 18.
25. Ebert, "More Papers Cutting Ties," p. 5.
26. Constitution of the Northland College Communications Commission, Inc., November 1, 1971.
27. Constitution and Bylaws of the Student Publishing Company of Northwestern University, revised 1961.

28. Articles of Incorporation of the *O'Collegian* Publishing Company, August 31, 1926.

29. Bylaws of the *Oregon Daily Emerald* Publishing Company, August 31, 1971.

30. Bylaws of the Student Publications Board, Inc., University of South Dakota.

31. Bylaws of Campus Publications, 1971, pp. 2–3.

32. Policies of the Board of Governors of State Colleges and Universities.

33. Excerpt of a statement by the University of Wisconsin Board of Regents, February 5, 1965.

34. Bylaws of the *Wisconsin Badger, Inc.,* 1966, p. 1.

35. Bylaws of the New *Daily Cardinal* Corporation, p. 2.

36. Dario Politella, ed., *The College Media Directory 1989* (New York: Oxbridge Communications, 1989).

37. Lillian L. Kopenhaver and Ronald E. Spielberger, "Are Independent College Papers Really Independent?" *College Media Review* (Spring 1989): pp. 5–7.

CHAPTER 3

1. Duscha and Fischer, *Campus Press,* p. 60.

2. Duscha and Fischer, *Campus Press,* pp. 66–69.

3. *College and University Reports,* No. 15.986.

4. Lillian L. Kopenhaver and Ronald E. Spielberger, "Student Media Profile," *College Media Review* (Spring/Summer 1987): pp. 13–16.

CHAPTER 5

1. Proposal adopted in 1970 by the North Dakota Board of Higher Education.

2. Ind. Code Ann., 23–7–1.1–4 (Burns 1972 & Supp. 1980).

3. See Ohio Rev. Codes, 1702.12 (1979).

4. Ind. Code Ann., 23–7–1.1–18 (Burns 1972 & Supp. 1980).

5. See Ky. Rev. Stat. Ann., 273.247 (Baldwin 1980).

6. Ind. Code Ann., 23–7–1.1–21 (Burns 1972 & Supp. 1980).

7. Ind. Code Ann., 23–7–1.1–8 (Burns 1972 & Supp. 1980).

8. Ibid.

9. See Ohio Rev. Codes, 1702.30 (1979) and Ky. Rev. Stat. Ann., 273.247 (Baldwin 1980).

10. See, e.g., In re First National Bank, 23 F. Supp. 255 (E.D. Ill. 1938); Minton v. Cavaney, 56 Cal. 2d 546, 364 P.2d 473, 15 Cal. Rptr. 641 (1961); and Kilpatrick Bros., Inc. v. Poynter, 205 Kan. 787, 473 P.2d 44 (1970); but see Critzer v. Oban, 52 Wash. 2d 440, 326 P.2d 53 (1958).

11. See, e.g., Associated Vendors, Inc. v. Oakland Meat Co., 210 Cal. App. 2d 825, 25 Cal. Rptr. 806 (1962) and African Metals Corp. v. Bullowa, 288 N.Y.

12. See Ind. Code Ann., 23–7–1.1–36 (Burns 1972 & Supp. 1980) and Ky. Rev. Stat. Ann., 273.367 (Baldwin 1980).
13. See Code 508(a) and Treas. Reg. 1.508–1(a)(2), (3).
14. Treas. Reg. 1.508–1(a)(2).
15. Rev. Proc. 80–25, 1980–1 C.B. 667.
16. Ibid. See 7 Ref. Tax Coordinator D-4011 (1980).
17. See Treas. Reg. 1.512(a)–1(a).
18. See Treas. Reg. 1.513–1(a).
19. See Code 6033(a)(1).
20. See Boettcher, 337 T.M., Exempt Organizations – Exemption and Filing Requirements A-59 (1976 & Supp., 1981).
21. Ibid. See, e.g., Ind. Code Ann. 6–21–3–20 (Burns 1972 & Supp. 1980); generally exempts from gross income tax income received by a not-for-profit corporation organized and operated exclusively for religious, charitable, scientific, literary, educational, or civic purposes.

CHAPTER 7

1. Herman Estrin, "The Collegiate Press: Irresistible, Irreverent, but Relevant," *Scholastic Editor,* May 1973, pp. 8–11.

CHAPTER 10

1. "The Tenth Alexander Meiklejohn Award," *AAUP Bulletin,* Summer 1968, pp. 162–63.
2. "The Eleventh Alexander Meiklejohn Award," *AAUP Bulletin,* Summer 1968, pp. 251–52.
3. Data in full in the Student Press in America Archives.
4. Excerpt of Statement by the University of Wisconsin Board of Regents, February 5, 1965.

CHAPTER 11

1. "Publications," *Bill of Student Rights,* Louisiana State University and Agricultural and Mechanical College, pp. 5, 6.
2. Bylaws of the Board of Student Publications of Wichita State University.
3. Publications Board Charter of Portland State College, July 17, 1967.
4. Office of the President, "The Student Publications Policy Committee," Kent State University, April 25, 1966.

CHAPTER 12

1. Bob Hendrickson. "Variables in Organization and Free Press in Private Colleges," College Media Adviser Convention Presentation, The School of the Ozarks, Point Lookout, MO, 1987.
2. Andres Ciofalo, "Private Schools and Press Freedom," *College Media Review* 27, nos. 1, 3 (Fall-Winter 1988).

CHAPTER 13

1. Comments about the development of the First Amendment and its scope are summarized from the Ingelhart book *Freedom for the College Student Press*.
2. John David Reed, "Toward a Theory of the First Amendment for the College Press," unpublished doctoral dissertation, Southern Illinois University, Carbondale, IL; 1985. (Reed's notes have been modified.)
3. "Poses, the Bugle Still Calls," *Quill* 93 (June 1985).
4. Yench v. Stockmar, 483 F.2d 820 (10th Cir. 1973).
5. Lee v. Board of Regents of State Colleges, 441 F.2d 1257 (7th Cir. 1971).
6. Dickey v. Alabama State Board of Education, 273 F. Supp. 613, 618 (M.D. Ala. 1967) *dismissed as moot sub nom.* and Troy State University v. Dickey, 402 F.2d 515 (5th Cir. 1968).
7. Joyner v. Whiting, 477 F.2d 456, 462 (4th Cir. 1973).
8. "Right to endorse at Issue in Humboldt State Lawsuit," *Student Press Law Center Report* (Spring 1985): pp. 6–7.
9. "Court: Public College Paper Can't Reject Abortion Ads," *Editor and Publisher* 114 (October 10, 1981): p. 20.
10. Yench v. Stockmar, 483 F.2d 820.
11. Bazaar v. Fortune, 476 F.2d 570 (5th Cir. 1973), *aff'd as modified en banc,* 489 F. 2d 225 (1973), *cert. denied,* 416 U.S. 995 (1974) (emphasis added).
12. Ibid. at 580 (emphasis added).
13. Antonelli v. Hammond, 308 F. Supp. 1329 (D. Mass. 1970).
14. Schiff v. Williams, 519 F.2d 257 (5th Cir. 1975).
15. See, e.g., Antonelli v. Hammond, 308 F. Supp. 1329; Trujillo v. Love, 322 F. Supp. 1266 (D. Colo. 1970).
16. See, e.g., Korn v. Elkins, 317 F. Supp. 138 (D. Md. 1970); Johnson v. Board of Junior College Dist. No. 508, 334 N.E.2d 442 (Ill. App. Ct. 1975); Kiluma v. Wayne State University, 250 N.W.2d 81 (Mich. App. Ct. 1977).
17. *Bazaar II,* 489 F.2d 225.
18. See, e.g., Lee v. Board of Regents, 441 F.2d 1257; Lace v. University of Vermont, 303 A.2d 475 (Vt. 1973); Larson v. Board of Regents of the University of Nebraska, 204 N.W.2d 568 (Neb. 1973); Joyner v. Whiting, 477 F.2d 456.
19. *Dickey,* 273 F. Supp. 613.
20. Ibid.
21. 308 F. Supp. at 1329 (emphasis added).

22. 476 F.2d 570.

23. See Reed, chap. 1.

24. *Law of the Student Press* (1985), p. 17. See also Notes, "Public Forum Theory in the Educational Setting: The First Amendment and the Student Press," U. Ill. L.F. (1979): pp. 895–99.

25. See, e.g., Antonelli v. Hammond, 308 F. Supp. 1336 and Mazart v. State, 441 N.Y.S. 2d 600, 606–607 (N.Y. Ct. Cl. 1981).

26. 393 U.S. 503, 514 (1969).

27. 410 U.S. 667, 671 (1971).

28. 403 U.S. 713 (1971).

29. 420 U.S. 546, 553 (1975).

30. Trager and Plopper, "Public Forum Theory in the Educational Setting: From the Schoolhouse Gate to the Student Press," paper presented to Association for Education in Journalism, Annual Meeting, Seattle, Washington, August 21, 1978.

31. Cox v. New Hampshire, 312 U.S. 569, 576 (1941).

32. 410 U.S. at 670.

33. Widmar v. Vincent, 454 U.S. 263, 277 (1981).

34. Simpson, "Simpson's Reply: Study the Law!" *Student Press Law Center Report* 3 (Fall 1980): p. 5 (emphasis added).

35. Notes, "Public Forum Theory," at 880 (emphasis added).

36. Organization for a Better Austin v. Keefe, 402 U.S. 415 (1971).

37. United States Postal Service v. Council of Greenburgh Civic Association, 453 U.S. 114 (1981).

38. United States Postal Service v. Council of Greenburgh Civic Association, 453 U.S. 114 (1981).

39. Perry Educational Association v. Perry Local Educators' Association, 460 U.S. 37 (1983).

40. Ibid. at 49.

41. Lehman v. City of Shaker Heights, 418 U.S. 298, 306 (Douglas, J., concurring).

42. *Southeastern Promotions,* 420 U.S. at 563 (Douglas, J., dissenting).

43. Simpson, "Simpson's Reply."

44. Notes, "Public Forum Theory," at 880 n.9.

45. See, e.g., *Dickey,* 273 F. Supp. 613; *Trujillo,* 322 F. Supp. 1266; *Antonelli,* 308 F. Supp. 1329; *Joyner,* 477 F.2d 456.

46. Claypool, "Forum Theory: Why Administrators Are Not the 'Publisher,' " *Student Press Law Center Report* 2 (Fall 1979): p. 46.

47. 440 F.2d 133, 135 (9th Cir. 1971).

48. 418 U.S. 298.

49. 412 U.S. 94 (1973) and 104 S.Ct. 3106 (1984).

50. 418 U.S. 241 (1974).

51. Trager and Plopper, "Public Forum Theory," at 20.

52. *Law of the Student Press,* at 5.

53. Fager, "Ownership and Control of the Student Press: A First Amendment Analysis," paper presented to Association for Education in Journalism, Annual Meeting, August 2, 1976, College Park, MD.

54. Notes, "Public Forum Theory," at 913.

55. Mississippi Gay Alliance v. Goudelock, Civ. No. EC-74-28-K, 8 (N.D.

Miss. 1974), *aff'd,* 536 F.2d 1073 (5th Cir. 1976), *cert. denied,* 430 U.S. 982 (1977).

56. Ibid. at 12 (emphasis added).

57. Ibid. at 11.

58. 418 U.S. at 258.

59. A. Meiklejohn, *Free Speech and Its Relation to Self-Government* (1948), p. 24.

60. 418 U.S. at 258.

61. Trager and Dickerson, *College Student Press Law* 2 (1979).

62. 418 P.2d 404, 412 (Ariz. App. Ct. 1966).

63. 319 U.S. 624, 637 (1943).

64. Ingelhart, *Freedom for the College Student Press* 72 (1985).

65. 412 U.S. at 115.

66. Hudgens, 424 U.S. at 520.

67. Trager and Dickerson, *College Student Press Law,* at 11.

68. 412 U.S. at 162 (Douglas J., concurring).

69. Cornelius v. NAACP Legal Defense and Educational Fund, Inc., 473 U.S. 788 (1985).

CHAPTER 14

1. Dario Politella, Preface, *Directory of the Student Press,* 3d biennial ed. (New York: Oxbridge Publishing Company).

2. John Ciardi, "Student Publications and the Tufts Plan," *Saturday Review,* September 11, 1965, pp. 20–22.

3. Annette Gibbs, "The Student Press: Guidelines for College Administrators," *Journal of NAWDC* (Summer 1971): pp. 159–61.

4. *The College Media Directory 1989* (New York: Oxbridge Communications, 1989); see "Overview" pages.

INDEX